MW00933730

God's Girls 105:

Homemaking

By Meredith Curtis

Copyright © 2016 Meredith L. Curtis

All rights reserved.

Published by Powerline Productions/Kingdom Building Services, Inc.

Printed by CreateSpace, an Amazon Company.

All Photos and clipart © Sarah Jeffords, Josh Nolette, Sarah Joy Curtis, Meredith Curtis, Laura Nolette, and licensees/Used with permission/All rights reserved. Sewing & Craft Instructions © Lauran Nolette/Used with permission.

Thank you, Laura Nolette, for all the wonderful sewing and craft instructions, you are a blessing!

All rights reserved. No part of this publication may be reproduced, stored in a retrieval system, or transmitted, in any form, or by any means—digital, mechanical, photocopying, recording, or otherwise—without prior permission from the author.

ISBN-13: 978-1973736257

DEDICATION

This class is dedicated to Shine with love!

Table of Contents

Homemaking Course Requirements

Textbooks

The Holy Bible

Hidden Art of Homemaking by Edith Scaheffer

Jesus, Fill My Herat & Home by Meredith Curtis

Optional Living Books

Welcome Home by Emilie Barnes

Managing to Be Free by Shirley Daniels & Marian Jones Clark

Beautiful Home on a Budget by Emilie Barnes & Yoli Brogger

Building Her House Well by Alice Reynolds Flower

All The Way Home by Mary Pride

The Stay At Home Mom by Donna Otto

Home God's Design by Miriam Huffman Rockness

A Woman and Her Home by Ella May Miller

Assignments:

- Memorize Proverbs 31:10-31
- Complete *Jesus Fill My Heart & Home Bible Study* and Discuss each Lesson with Mom
- Read *Hidden Art of Homemaking* and Accompanying Lesson for each Chapter with Mom
- Read All Articles in this Book & Discuss with Mom
- Sewing Projects: Hand Stitching, Pillowcase, Apron, Napkins (Serger), Dress
- Cooking; Casseroles, Crock Pot Meals, Holiday Dishes, Turkey, International Dishes
- Baking: Cookies, Bread
- Collect Recipes for Recipe Box
- Cake Decorating
- Candy Making
- Make a Family Worship Songbook
- Paint a Picture Thomas Kinkade-Style using Light Expressively

- Grocery Shop with Mom's Grocery Money
- Grocery Shop with ½ Mom's Grocery Money
- Laundry Project
- Make a Practical Schedule for Different Homemakers (Rachel, Esther, Lydia)
- Learn to Organize, Tidy, & Clean
- Organize & Lead a Family Cleaning Day
- Organize, Tidy, Clean, & Decorate Your Room
- Learn to Decorate
- Dream House Project
- Make a Welcome Wreath
- Decorate House for Christmas
- Wrap Christmas Presents Creatively
- Plant a Garden
- Arrange Flowers
- With Nutrition & Artistry in Mind, Create a Weekly Menu
- Make Jam
- Write a Poem about Homemaking
- Create & Perform a Skit about Homemaking
- Choose Perfect Gifts
- Make Birthday Special/Plan a Birthday Party
- Take Photographs/Store & Display Photographs
- Scrapbook
- Make a Proverbs 31 Booklet for Children
- Fantastic Family Fun Night Project
- Plan & Build a Timeless Wardrobe/Accessorize
- Care for Clothing & Accessories
- Spend Time with Someone from Another Generation
- Serve an Elderly Person
- Write an Essay on "Homemaking: A Noble Career"
- Plan & Hostess a Mother's Day Tea

Grading:

To get a **C** grade, complete all work like it is just an assignment. Demonstrate adequate skills and character growth.

To get an **A** grade, complete all work cheerfully and with excellence. Demonstrate growth in Jesus in attitude, actions, service and speech.

Homemaking Syllabus/Assignment Check-Off

Assignments   Completed

September Week One Meet with Mom

Recite Proverbs 31
Go over "Homemaking Syllabus" & Pass Out Books
Discuss Hidden Art & Homemaking
Hand Sewing
Start Recipe Files

September Week One Home

Copy Proverbs 31
Jesus, Fill My Heart & Home Lesson 1: Masks, Makeovers, or the Natural Look
Read "Homemaking: A Lifetime Career Choice"
Read "Home is...."
Read *Hidden Art of Homemaking* Ch. 1 (First Artist)
Read & Do "Hidden Art of Homemaking: First Artist"

September Week Two Meet with Mom

Recite Proverbs 31
Sewing: Make Pillowcase

September Week Two Home

Copy Proverbs 31
Jesus, Fill My Heart & Home Lesson 2: Making Ourselves at Home in His Presence
Read *Hidden Art of Homemaking* Ch. 2 (What is Hidden Art?)
Read & Do "Hidden Art of Homemaking: What is Hidden Art?"
Add Recipes to Recipe Card File

September Week Three Meet with Mom

Recite Proverbs 31
Sewing: Pillowcase

September Week Three & Four Home

Copy Proverbs 31
Jesus, Fill My Heart & Home Lesson 3: Am I Praying Loud Enough for God to Hear?
Read *Hidden Art of Homemaking* Ch. 3: Music
Read & Do "Hidden Art of Homemaking: Music"

Hidden Art of Music: Put together a Family Worship Song Book

Read "Casseroles: Whole Meal in One Dish"

Cook a Casserole

Cook a Casserole

Optional: Read *Welcome Home* by Emilie Barnes

Optional: Book Review Sheet

October Week One Meet with Mom

Recite Proverbs 31

Hidden Art of Music: Share Family Worship Song Books

October Week One Home

Copy Proverbs 31

Jesus, Fill My Heart & Home Lesson 4: Abiding in Prayer

Read *Hidden Art of Homemaking* Ch. 4 (Painting, Sculpting, Sketching)

Read & Do "Hidden Art of Homemaking: Painting, Sculpting, Sketching"

Read Christian Artist Thomas Kinkade & His Paintings

Go Grocery Shopping

October Week Two Meet with Mom

Recite Proverbs 31

Hidden Art of Painting: Paint a home Thomas Kinkaid Style

with Light Shining through the Windows

October Week Two Home

Copy Proverbs 31

Jesus, Fill My Heart & Home Lesson 5: Walking & Dancing with Jesus

Read Family Finances & the Economics Cycle

Go Grocery Shopping with Half Money

Read Secrets Every Homemaker Should Know

Add Recipes to Recipe Card File

October Week Three Meet with Mom

Recite Proverbs 31

Sewing All Day Workshop: Make Apron

October Week Three & Four Home

Copy Proverbs 31

Jesus, Fill My Heart & Home Lesson 6: Abiding in His Spirit

Read "How to Do Laundry: Sort, Remove Stains, Wash, Dry, Fold, Put Away"

Fill Out "How We Do Laundry" Chart

Do the Entire Family's Laundry with Mom

Read "Time Management for the Homemaker"

Read "A Homemaker's Schedule"

Read "Crockpot Cooking: Whole Meal in One Pot"

Cook a Crockpot Meal

Cook a Crockpot Meal

Optional: Read *Managing to Be Free* by Shirley Daniels

Optional: Book Review Sheet

November Week One Meet with Mom

Recite Proverbs 31

Make Laundry Soap

Discuss Proverbs 31 & Scheduling & Time Management

November Week One Home

Copy Proverbs 31

Jesus, Fill My Heart & Home Lesson 7: Heaven, Our Real Home

Read "Hidden Art of Cleaning"

Read "How to Organize"

Read "How to Tidy"

Read "How to Clean"

Tidy & Clean Family House

Make a House Cleaning Plan & Administrate for Family Cleaning Day

Make a Family Cleaning Schedule

November Week Two Meet with Mom

Recite Proverbs 31

Discuss Hidden Art of Cleaning

Go Over Homemaking Skills Checklist Together

Make Homemade Lip Gloss

November Week Two Home

Copy Proverbs 31

Jesus, Fill My Heart & Home Lesson 8: Home, a Reflection of Heaven: A Prepared Place

Read "My Room: A Haven of Peace, A Reflection of Me"

Organize, Tidy, & Clean Your Room

Rearrange & Decorate Your Room

November Week Three Meet with Mom

Recite Proverbs 31

Discuss Your Room

Serging All Day Workshop: Make Holiday Napkins (Christmas or Thanksgiving)

November Week Three & Four Home

Copy Proverbs 31
Jesus, Fill My Heart & Home Lesson 9: How God Decorates & How We Decorate
Read *Hidden Art of Homemaking* Ch. 5: Interior Decorating
Read & Do "Hidden Art of Homemaking: Interior Decorating"
Read "Architectural Styles" & "Decorating Styles" & "Color Combinations"
Read "Holiday Recipes & Family Favorites" & "How to Cook a Turkey"
List Favorite Holiday Recipes
Cooking: Prepare the Turkey for Thanksgiving
Add Recipes to Recipe Card File
Optional: Read *Beautiful Home on a Budget* by Emilie Barns & Yoli Brogger
Optional: Book Review Sheet

December Week One Meet with Mom

Recite Proverbs 31
Discuss Principles of Interior Design
Discuss What You Like & Why (Architecture, Decorating, Styles, Colors)
Make a Wreath, Wall Hanging, or Plague

December Week One Home

Copy Proverbs 31
Read "How to Wrap Presents Creatively"
Read & Do "Dream House Project"

December Week Two Meet with Mom

Recite Proverbs 31
Make an Ornament
Share Dream House Projects

December Week Two Home

Copy Proverbs 31
Jesus, Fill My Heart & Home Lesson 10: Dwelling Place & Nurturing Center
Decorate Your House for Christmas
Wrap Presents Creatively
Read "Cake Decorating 101"
Bake Roll Out Cookies
Bake Drop Cookies

December Week Three Meet with Mom

Recite Proverbs 31

Hands-On Cake Decorating Workshop

December Week Three & Four Home

Copy Proverbs 31

Read *Hidden Art of Homemaking* Ch. 6: Gardening

Read & Do "Hidden Art of Homemaking: Gardening"

Add Recipes to Recipe Card File

Shopping with Mom: Choose Material & Pattern for Dress

Optional: Read *Building Her House Well* by Alice Reynolds Flower

Optional: Book Review Sheet

January Week One Meet with Mom

Recite Proverbs 31

Start Seedlings for Spring Garden

Plan Garden Together to Plant when the Weather Warms Up

Sewing All Day Workshop: Cut Out Pattern for Dress

January Week One Home

Copy Proverbs 31

Jesus, Fill My Heart & Home Lesson 11: Jesus Invites Himself Over

Read "How to Arrange Flowers 101"

Read "Candy Making 101"

Make Candy

January Week Two Meet with Mom

Recite Proverbs 31

Silk Flower Arranging & Make a Silk Flower Arrangement

Make Candy

January Week Two Home

Copy Proverbs 31

Read *Hidden Art of Homemaking* Ch. 7: Flower Arrangement

Read & Do "Hidden Art of Homemaking: Flower Arrangement & Still Life"

Read and "Choosing The Perfect Gift"

January Week Three Meet with Mom

Recite Proverbs 31
Create Your Own Still Life

January Week Three & Four Home

Copy Proverbs 31
Read *Hidden Art of Homemaking* Ch. 8: Food
Read & Do "Hidden Art of Homemaking: Food"
Read "How to Bake Bread the Old-Fashioned Way"
Bake Bread the Old-Fashioned Way
Add Recipes to Recipe Card File
Optional: Read *All The Way Home* by Mary Pride
Optional: Book Review Sheet

February Week One Meet with Mom

Recite Proverbs 31
Make St. Valentine's Day Cards
Sewing All Day Workshop: Dress

February Week One Home

Copy Proverbs 31
Read "Nutrition 101"
Read "Menu Planning" & Plan a Week's Menu

February Week Two Meet with Mom

Recite Proverbs 31
Discuss Nutrition & Menu Planning
Share Menus

February Week Two Home

Copy Proverbs 31
Read *Hidden Art of Homemaking* Ch. 9: Writing/Prose/Poetry
Read & Do "Hidden Art of Homemaking: Writing/Prose/Poetry"
Read "How to Make Jam"
Write a Poem about Homemaking

February Week Three Meet with Mom

Recite Proverbs 31
Go Strawberry Picking
Make Strawberry Jam

February Week Three & Four Home

Copy Proverbs 31
Read *Hidden Art of Homemaking* Ch. 10: Drama
Read & Do "Hidden Art of Homemaking: Drama"
Create a Skit on Homemaking & Videotape
Read "How to Take Great Photographs"
Add Recipes to Recipe Card File
Optional: Read *Stay at Home Mom* by Donna Otto
Optional: Book Review Sheet

March Week One Meet with Mom

Recite Proverbs 31
Perform Homemaking Skit
Sewing All Day Workshop: Dress

March Week One Home

Copy Proverbs 31
Jesus, Fill My Heart & Home Lesson 12: Welcome Center & Celebration Center"
Read "How to Store & Display Photos"
Read "How to Scrapbook"

March Week Two Meet with Mom

Recite Proverbs 31
Discuss Celebrations & Hospitality
Scrapbook Together

March Week Two Home

Copy Proverbs 31
Read "How to Make Birthdays Special"
Read "Birthday Party Ideas"
Read & Do "Making Birthdays Special Project"
Read & Do "Proverbs 31 Books for Little Girls Project"

March Week Three Meet with Mom

Recite Proverbs 31
Share Birthday Party Ideas
Share Proverbs 31 Booklets

March Week Three & Four Home

Copy Proverbs 31
Read *Hidden Art of Homemaking* Ch. 10: Creative Recreation
Read & Do "Hidden Art of Homemaking: Creative Recreation"
Read & Do "Fantastic Family Night Fun Project"
Plan &Hostess a Family Night (menu, activities, etc.)
Search for Foreign Recipe to Try
Search for Foreign Recipe to Try
Add Recipes to Recipe Card File
Optional: Read *Home God's Design* by Miriam Huffman Rockness
Optional: Book Review Sheet

April Week One Meet with Mom

Recite Proverbs 31
Discuss Creative Recreation & Family Night Experiences
Scrapbook
Sewing All Day Workshop: Dress

April Week One Home

Copy Proverbs 31
Read *Hidden Art of Homemaking* Ch. 11: Clothing
Read & Do "Hidden Art of Homemaking: Clothing"
Read & Do "Build My Wardrobe Project"
Read "How to Shop for Clothes"
Read "Clothing a Household"

April Week Two Meet with Mom

Recite Proverbs 31
Discuss Clothing
Put Together Outfits

April Week Two Home

Copy Proverbs 31
Experiment with Accessorizing
Read "Care of Clothing, Shoes, & Accessories"

April Week Three Meet with Mom

Recite Proverbs 31
Discuss Care of Clothing, Shoes, & Accessories
Put Together Outfits & Accessorize

April Week Three & Four Home

Copy Proverbs 31

Read *Hidden Art of Homemaking* Ch. 13: Integration

Read & Do "Hidden Art of Homemaking: Integration"

Spend Time with Another Generation & Write Blog Post about Experience

Read & Do "Caring for the Elderly Project"

Add Recipes to Recipe Card File

Optional: Read *A Woman and Her Home*

Optional: Book Review Sheet

May Week One Meet with Mom

Recite Proverbs 31

Role Play Caring for Elderly & Sick

Read Blog Posts Aloud

Sewing All Day Workshop: Dress

May Week One Home

Copy Proverbs 31

Write an Essay entitled: "Homemaking, a Noble Career"

Plan & Hostess a Mother's Day Tea

May Week Two Meet with Mom

Recite Proverbs 31

Homemaker Panel

May Week Two Home

Copy Proverbs 31

Read *Hidden Art of Homemaking* Ch. 14: Environment

Read & Do "Hidden Art of Homemaking: Environment"

Questions & Answers about Homemaking

List 10 People Who Create a Positive Environment. How Do They Do It?

May Week Three Meet with Mom

Recite Proverbs 31

Fashion Show with Dresses You Made

Welcome to God's Girls Homemaking

What a joy to walk in God's calling as woman. We have the privilege of bringing forth life in our bodies one day. We nurture, comfort, encourage, offer hope, and point others to Jesus. Like Mary, the sister of Lazarus, we sit at Jesus' feet and soak up His wisdom and love. When Christ Jesus calls, "Who will follow Me?" We God's Girls Respond, "We will!" We surrender to the Lord in all areas of their lives: purity, servanthood, love, self-control, and disciplines. While the world is changing after the lies of satan and falling into the traps of the devil, we boldly trust Jesus and follow after Him. It's His way, His Word, His plan.

God's Girls is a series for building godly character, practical wisdom, and life skills in young women's lives. These classes are great for girls of all ages, including gals in high school who need preparation to become the wives, mothers, homemakers, and entrepreneurs. God's Girls character classes include Bible assignments, living books to read, essays to write, and other projects designed to impart Truth they can pass on to others.

The secret to the success of these classes is the weekly meetings with Mom (or mentor). All homework should be gone over and time spent in conversation, Bible study, and prayer when you get together for Mom time or co-op class. We have also used this book in a co-op setting. Instead of meeting with their mothers, girls meet in a small group with a godly woman/mentor/teacher.

The fourth week meeting is left for fun with Mom or co-op group. You can sew, bake, shop, play games, work on a project, go out to eat, or engage in any other wholesome activity that you both enjoy.

Directions for God's Girls Assignments

In addition to completing the assignments in this book, you will be reading *Hidden Art of Homemaking* by Edith Schaeffer and *Jesus, Fill My Heart & Home Bible Study*. The lessons are spread out throughout the whole year so that the truths in the book and Bible study will sink deep into your heart.

Books & Book Review Sheets

There is an optional book on homemaking to read each month. Pray before you sit down to read each time and ask God to help you to have discernment about what is true and how the principles in the book can apply to your life. After you read each book, you will fill out a simple book review sheet.

Blog Post

You will write a blog post about spending time with another generation. A blog post is short, with shorter sentences, and straight to the point. Photographs or illustrations are important, too.

Essay

You will write an essay entitled "Homemaking, A Noble Career." Think about all you have learned over the past year about homemaking. What is one thing you want to share with others? Create a thesis statement that will guide your essay. Make it encouraging for your audience. Make sure you choose an audience.

Booklets

Booklets are made for young children to read and understand God's plan for growing up to be a good homemaker. You can be as creative as you want to be as long as your booklet is easy to understand. Read it aloud to a child to see if they "get it."

Think carefully about Proverbs 31: 10-31 and how you can explain them to young children. Keep in mind your audience and make sure your pictures are bright and colorful—young children love bright colors.

You can also make a video if you want to. My daughter, Shine, liked to make videos for this assignment in addition to the booklet.

Hands-On Fun

This is course is almost all hands-on activities to prepare you to be a homemaker: cooking, baking sewing, photography, scrapbooking, candy making, floral arranging, organizing, cleaning, decorating, gift wrapping, serving others, and planning a Mother's Day tea. I hope you enjoy everything!

Each of my daughters took this class and they loved it! Enjoy the fun!

Lists and Charts

Many times, I will ask you to fill out a chart or list to brainstorm for an assignment. That's because I am trying to build in you the helpful habit of jotting down ideas.

If you have any questions or confusion, email me, **Meredith@powerlinecc.com**

September: Home Sweet Home

Memorize Proverbs 31

"Homemaking: A Lifetime Career Choice"

"Home Sweet Home"

Jesus, Fill My Heart & Home Bible Study

Hidden Art of Homemaking

Sew a Pillowcase

Optional: *Welcome Home* Book Review

(Meet with Mom weekly)

Week One Meet with Mom

Pass out books and Bible study. The focus is on being filled with the Presence of Jesus and bringing His Presence into our home. We will be learning many skills this year, but more importantly, we will focus on imitating Jesus, who created the perfect home, Heaven.

Go Over Plan for Year

- September through October: Abiding in Jesus through worship, prayer, & Bible. Imitating God as an Artist, Music, Painting, Sketching. Make a Family Worship Book, Paint, Sew a Pillowcase, Sew an Apron, Casseroles, Crockpot Meals, Laundry.
- November through December: Our Home in Heaven, Home Organization, Cleaning, Schedules, Interior Decorating, Dream House & Garden Project, Serging Christmas Napkins, Holiday Cooking, Baking Cookies, Cake Decorating, Gardens.
- January through February: Nurturing Center, Dwelling Place, Plant Garden Seedlings, Flower Arranging, Still Life, Candy Making, Food, Nutrition, Grocery Project, Bake Bread, Sew Dress, Cards & Gift Project.
- March through May: Welcome Center, Celebration Center, Drama, Recreation, Clothing, Integration, Environment, Photography, Scrapbooking, Birthday, Proverbs 31 Booklet, Work on Dress, Homemaking Skit, Wardrobe Project, Family Night Project, Care of Elderly & Sick, Hostess a Mother's Day Tea.

Work on Different Hand Stitching: Thread a Needle, Make a Knot, Basting Stitch, Running Stitch, Back Stitch, Hemming Stitch, Overcast Stitch, Slip Stitch

Make Recipe Files

- Purchase a beautiful recipe box together, OR
- Make your own. Purchase a wooden box from Hobby Lobby® or other craft store. Paint and decorate as desired with shells, flowers, ribbons, coins, or buttons, etc.

Prayer Focus:

- Year Ahead
- Mother/Daughter Relationship
- Filled with His Presence
- Growing in Homemaking Skills

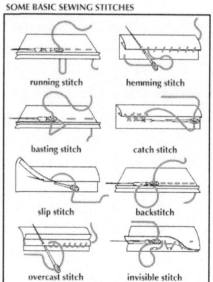

SOME BASIC SEWING STITCHES

running stitch • hemming stitch
basting stitch • catch stitch
slip stitch • backstitch
overcast stitch • invisible stitch

Week One Home

Memorize Proverbs 31:10-31

Write Proverbs 31:10-31 in the version of your choice. I recommend NASB or NKJ or ESV. Then say the passage aloud.

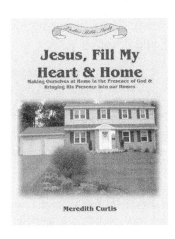

Jesus, Fill My Heart & Home Lesson 1

"Masks, Makeovers, or the Natural Look"

Read and Answer Questions

Homemaking, A Lifetime Career Choice: A Word to Moms & Teens

My grandmother lived in a time where women stayed home and took care of the home and family. She was honored for her lovely home, delicious cooking, and well-mannered children. Like her mother and grandmother before her, Louise embraced the lifetime career of homemaker with a cheerful heart. Though one of the few women to graduate from college, she still chose to be home and care for her family.

My mother started out as a homemaker in the sixties, but the Woman's Liberation Movement came like a storm through our lives in the seventies. Suddenly, the sacred calling of women working at home became suspect. Could a woman possibly be "fulfilled" if she stayed at home cleaning and wiping running noses? Society began to push women into the workplace. This push came from the media, public schools, books, and even from churches.

Swimming Upstream in the Eighties

When I graduated from college in 1984, it was a time in history when motherhood and homemaking were mocked and ridiculed. The idea of an intelligent young woman devoting her life to serving her husband, raising her children, and "creating" a home for her family was distasteful at best, a "waste of her time, brain, and skills." Young girls were discouraged from homemaking as a career, and homemaking tasks were thought of as "boring" and "unnecessary." Girls that wanted to grow up to be homemakers had to keep it a secret or they were labeled "OUT of IT!" and "Stupid!"

Nineties and the "Mommy Track"

In the nineties, women began to wake up and realize that they'd been tricked into trying to "do it all" and attempt the "supermom" role of bringing home the bacon and frying it up in the pan. They realized that they had been lied to by the writers, professors, teachers, and movie stars. You can't really "do it all!" And worst of all, they were missing their children terribly, especially their babies.

Women began to take the "mommy track," which meant taking a break from their career to enjoy their babies. Of course, as soon as the kids were in school, there was just no excuse to stay home anymore, so it was back to work!

The Twenty-First Century

While some people mock and ridicule motherhood, most people in the world still admire women who care for their home and family.

I do notice that while men are often portrayed as doing traditional homemaker roles, advertizing for homemaking products still targets women. Why is that? Even if women have to work outside the home, they are still the ones who long to create a beautiful refuge from the world for their loved ones. Women around the world care about their family's health, nutritional needs, and clothing. Women lead the way in planning celebrations for life's most important events from birthdays to holidays, to graduations to weddings.

Still girls are pushed into the work force by the media, public schools, and well-meaning family members who are concerned about rising divorce rates.

Yet many girls of today want to stay home because they know someone who is a homemaker and find their life very attractive. OR…they sense a call from God. Yes, God still does call women to the lifetime career of homemaking.

Homemaking: A Career?

"Train the younger women… to be busy at home" (Titus 2:4-5 NIV ©1979).

What does homemaking have to do with discipling your teenage daughters? If you are a teenager, what does it have to do with growing in Christ? Is that a question going through your mind as we begin this course? Let's see if I can answer that for you…

Our Heavenly Father, the Creator and King of the Universe, sees homemaking as a high calling, a role of dignity and purpose; a productive and fruitful way to spend our lives serving Him. To the Lord it is not even optional. It is our King who commands us as young mother to be "busy at home" (Titus 2:5); and who gives the definition of a valuable wife in Proverbs 31 describing a skilled and productive homemaker.

We learn from the Bible that the role of a homemaker includes: loving, respecting, being faithful to, submitting to, helping, bringing good to our husbands; loving, training, teaching, disciplining our children; nutrition and food preparation; interior decorating; gardening; production and care of clothing; hospitality; skilled work with our hands in the area of arts/crafts/sewing; managing money; giving to the poor; home business/ministry; managing the household; and most importantly continuously cultivating a deep walk with Jesus.

Real Young Ladies Consider Homemaking

Consider the following scenarios and keep in mind that these girls (not their real names but nonetheless real friends of mine) are all Christians.

Valerie—Got a BS degree in Medical Technology but after her first baby was born she quit her job to stay at home. Her mother refused to talk to her for several months and for years ridiculed her. She put her degree to good use by homeschooling her children.

Cathy—(17) Thinks that homemaking is O.K. for some but she is too smart to "waste her brain."

Jacki—(17) Considers staying home one day with her babies (for the first year) but is afraid she will be bored—wants an "exciting career."

Kate—(17) Has a boyfriend that she would like to marry and would like to be a homemaker. However, there is tremendous pressure from her Christian mother not to "waste her life."

Debbie—(14) A homemaker at heart and desires to be one but her Christian mother wants her to be a brain surgeon so she can make a lot of money and hire a nanny. She really wants to please her mother so she is considering medicine.

Ellen—(18) With the support of her Christian parents, she is choosing her college degree major based on the fact that she wants to be a full-time homemaker.

Five of these girls were teens I met in church and only one of them had a heart for homemaking without discouragement from her family. Even Christian women are being sold a lie that success lies outside the home. You might ask: "Can a woman be fulfilling God's purpose by staying home and raising a family?"

God's Plan & Purpose &Homemaking

The truth is that homemaking is a calling, a privilege, and a command (Titus 2:3-5 and Proverbs 14:1). And God considers homemaking worthy of commendation (Proverbs 31 and I Timothy 5:9-10).

God's plan and purpose in the earth is to exalt Christ and to bring together a people (a family, a body) that knows and loves Jesus, and to knit them together and making them mature (as individuals and as a group) until they are ready to be presented to Jesus as a glorious bride. At which time Jesus will return to judge the earth and marry His bride, taking her home to Heaven to live forever and ever. That is what each of us are giving our live to—that is our purpose and reason to live—to fit

MEREDITH CURTIS

into what God is doing in the earth. So how does homemaking fit in?

1. Part of the people that God is bringing together for Jesus includes our little ones. Committing ourselves to being at home where we are able to nurture, discipline, love, and train our children (rather than a daycare provider) makes it possible to pass on our spiritual heritage to them and train them in the ways of the Lord.

2. When we are working outside the home, it is easy to have our *own* agenda and pursue our *own* personal goals. Homemaking makes it easier to follow the Lord together as a household with the Lord giving direction to the husband and confirming it through the wife. We can creatively support and help our husbands in their ministries, jobs, etc. We can serve God together as a family rather than individuals who each do "their own thing."

3. We are able to do a few things (like raising children) excellently rather than several things adequately or poorly. There is no such thing as a "Super Mom" who can excel in her career, be a great mom and supportive wife, have a wonderful home, link arms with others in the church, and reach out to the lost. That is a myth. A life like that usually saps our best years of strength and our best is given to those outside our family and God's purpose and plan.

4. Our marriage, family, and home can be a model for others and a relatable picture to our children and others of what spiritual realities, such as a personal relationship with Jesus, the Family of God and Heaven, are really like. This takes a commitment to plan and work hard to create a home that fits this description—it is a full time job!

5. Contentment in our role as a woman, wife, and mother is a beautiful testimony. Conversely, it also releases men to be men. As we come into our calling, it releases men to come into their callings of leadership and productivity. Strong men make strong leadership, which makes for a strong church (actually hastening the return of the Lord).

6. Our households are training ground for ministry in the church. An elder or overseer "must manage his own family well and see that his children obey him with proper respect. (If anyone does not know how to manage his own family, how can he take care of God's church?)" 1 Timothy 3:4-5 reminds us that church is a family too, so if we want to fulfill our calling in the church, we need to learn to effectively fulfill (an continue to fulfill) our calling as wives, mothers, and homemakers.

How can we impart these things to the teens? Moms, let's present homemaking as a lifetime career of purpose, dignity, productivity, fulfillment, and life changing value by modeling this truth with our lives. Let's be excellent at homemaking and understand why we are doing what we are doing. We can share our education, skills, and abilities (in a humble way, of course) and how we are using them in homemaking (our education was NOT a waste!). DON'T tell our daughters and friends they "should" be homemakers. DON'T preach. Just live a life that is worthy of imitation. Live a life that makes others want to live that way too.

Paul tells Titus how slaves can treat their masters to make the "teaching about God our Savior attractive." In the same way, let's conduct ourselves in such a way that it makes Good's teachings and commands attractive to the girls that we build friendships with and train in the Lord.

Teens, don't buy into the lie of this age. Come out and be separate! Make it your ambition to obey God's Word, rather than imitate the world. Look for positive role models in your own mom and other young and older homemakers. This earth is filled with godly women who serve their families as homemakers.

While many young couples worry about money, there are plenty of ways to earn extra money while staying home to care for your family as a top priority. If money is an issue for your family, talk to women who run their own businesses from home without letting those businesses take over their lives to get some ideas. The Proverbs 31 woman made linen garments and belts that she sells to merchants.

Many women help their husbands out with their businesses. Pattie keeps the financial records for her husband's lawn business. Carla sets appointments for her husband's pest control company. Felice does marketing for her husband's construction company.

It is important to keep in mind that God is the provider. He will provide through our husband's income if we will trust Him. Often we need to lower our expectations and learn to live more frugally. In fact, it seems that no matter how much money comes in, people feel like they need more. Surviving lean times together will help build financial disciplines that will enable you to save for the future and experience God's blessings.

Even if a woman works outside the home, her primary responsibility is to build and manage her home. Likewise, even if his wife works, the husband's job is to provide for his family.

Home Sweet Home

Home sweet home is so many different things to each one of us on this beautiful blue planet. Because we live in a fallen world, there is no perfect home on earth, but we can try to create a place of peace, joy, and safety for our families.

A HOME IS...

A Dwelling Place

Home is where you are comfortable, "feel at home," understood, appreciated, wanted, liked, and loved. When you walk in your home, you feel safe and at ease from conflicts of the world. You want to bring your friends, so you do, and they are welcomed in.

A School

Home is the place where parents model maturity and teach/train children until they are mature in daily life skills, character, emotional control, intellectual abilities, social graces, roles/responsibilities, interpersonal relationships, and developments of gifts/abilities, and, of course, their walk with the Lord. A home is filled with music, books, and other things that cultivate a love of learning.

A Nurturing Center

Home is a place where everyone in the family and even guests are nurtured carefully and lavishly. There is a loving, safe atmosphere with nutritious meals served creatively, dental care and good hygiene practiced, well-made clothing worn, fresh air provided and exercise enjoyed. Spirits are nurtured too with Bible reading, Bible teaching, prayer, worship, and family devotions that all take place on a regular basis.

A Happy Place

Fun! Laughter! Joy! Jokes! Celebrating God's Goodness! Beauty! Memories! Traditions! Hugs! Kisses! Cuddling! Affirmation! Music! Singing! Surprises! Home is a happy place where we laugh and make memories that last forever. ☺

A Hospital/Repair Shop

Home is a safe place, but when anyone is sick or wounded, home is where there is tender care for the sick, broken things are fixed, broken hearts mended, and crushed spirits healed. Home is a place for renewal and rest.

A Creative Productivity Center

We are not just a family of consumers, but we are producers! Gardening, baking, cooking, woodwork, crafts, sewing, painting, art projects, singing, playing musical instruments, writing songs/poetry/stories/books, and building machines are all ways that we produce with creativity and practicality.

A Hospitality Center

The Bible says to practice hospitality (Romans 12:13); do it regularly/repetitively. Opening our heart, life, and home to honor and serve others turns our home into a place of ministry. Linking arms with our church family and reaching out to the lost can happen in our homes through hospitality. We can show our love through baby and wedding showers, parties, game nights, dinners, brunches, hosting meetings, and having overnight company stay in our guest room.

A Ministry Center

God calls every Christian to a life of ministry. Your household/family is called to ministry in your home and from your home. Home is a place where love flows outward in giving to the poor; visiting and serving the elderly; caring for widows, orphans, single parents, and unwed pregnant girls; evangelistic outreach, discipling new believers; counseling; prayer and healing; and home group Bible studies.

A Prepared Place

A home is planned and prepared. It doesn't just happen. A clean, orderly, and organized home provides a sense of security. To make everything happen in a home that's supposed to happen requires a plan and a schedule. A wise homemaker sets goals for her husbands' needs and growing children's needs. The goals are met because plans are prayerfully made and carried through.

A Holy Place

Christ is honored in a Christian home. He is the Unseen Guest, the Good Shepherd, the One who is worshipped, the Healer, the Teacher, the Owner of everything, and the Master/King. Jesus calls the shots. He is obeyed. Jesus owns everything and every person in the home and the family behaves as His stewards, taking good care of one another and every possession. He is spoken of with respect and affection. His Word is the Law of the land. Everything is done with His strength to please and honor Him.

Even more our homes, like other temporary things, reflect eternity.

Reflections of Eternity

*"**Be** imitators of God, therefore, as dearly loved children and live a life of love, just as Christ loved us and gave Himself up for us as a fragrant offering and sacrifice to God"* (Ephesians 5:1 NIV ©1979).

We are called to be imitators of God with our lives, words, and attitudes. But, we also get to imitate God in some really special ways. Marriages, families, and homes are all temporary pictures of permanent things that we will experience forever in Heaven. ☺

Marriage

Our Marriage (a temporary relationship) can be a picture of the church's relationship with Jesus (a permanent forever one). See Ephesians 5:24-33 and Revelation 21:2. Our marriage can be a picture to our children and others of how Jesus loves us and how we honor and love Him.

Family

Our Family (a temporary group) can be a picture of the Family of God (a permanent group). See Ephesians 2:19-22 and Ephesians 3:14-15. As we love, forgive, honor, and serve one another, we model what life in the family of God should be—intimate, strongly committed with close ties that bind. We also need to be living this out in the local church where we are committed.

Home

Our Home (a temporary dwelling) can be a small-scale model of our Eternal Home: Heaven! (a permanent forever place). Philippians 3:20 tells us that our citizenship is in Heaven, our forever home! Our children can get an idea of what Heaven is like. Our home can be like heaven on earth.

"In my Father's house are many rooms; if it were not so, I would have told you. I am going there to prepare a place for you" (John 14:2 NIV ©1979).

Let's imitate Jesus who prepared a place for us in Heaven! Let's prepare a place for our family!

"One family and the children of that family can do marvelous things to affect the world or devastating things to destroy it. Hitler was one man born in one family. We could use many contrasting examples to emphasize that he old-fashioned saying 'The hand that rocks the cradle, rocks the world' is not just a group of quaint idiotic, romantic words—it just happens that they are true. The problem today is that people want to have computers rock the cradles, institutions take over from that point on, and have no human influence involved at all. What career is so important as to allow the family to become extinct? The family, which has continuity for not just one lifetime, but for generations, gives solidity and security and an environment that cannot be duplicated and which spreads in a wide circle.

"Who can make the family a career? The natural person provided with the attributes for that is the woman. The mother, who brings forth the child and can feed it for a year at her breasts, is versatile in the fantastic diversity of talents she can develop. In the rest of the book will be unfolded some of the variety in this career, and the excitement of the challenge in pioneering in an age when women are in danger of becoming extinct in the drive to be neuter. To be a mother and homemaker and an environmental expert in designing a place for the particular blend of people which will

be in your family—to grow and develop—is an amazing possibility. To be at the same time a wife and a companion, an interesting, growing, changing, developing person in the eyes of the man you married—not just two years nor twelve nor twenty nor thirty, but forty and fifty years—is an added portion of this career." (from *What is a Family?* By Edith Schaeffer)

"The wise woman builds her house, but with her own hands the foolish one tears hers down" (Prov. 14:1 NIV ©1979).

We have talked about homemaking as a calling and the home as a sacred place that reflects eternity. How do we build and manage our homes so that they impact all who dwell within and all who visit them?

How to Prepare Your Home

𝕬𝖇𝖎𝖉𝖊 in Christ

ABIDE! ABIDE! ABIDE! Carefully read, study, and meditate on John 15. This chapter teaches us that apart from Christ, we can do nothing. Learn to abide, or make yourself at home in, Jesus so that His Presence will fill you to overflowing.

It is when His Presence overflows in our life that we can bring His Presence into our homes to bless our families.

We are going to talk about Jesus being the First Artist. Wow! I love thinking of Jesus as an artist who paints rainbows across the skies and dots meadows with wildflowers. What a magnificent world He has made!

In this class, we are going to learn how to imitate Christ, to bring beauty and order into our lives and homes. So, get to know Jesus! The more you read about Him, pray to Him, and worship Him, the more you will fall in love with Him! ☺

Study God's Word

Study what God's Word has to say about the Home. II Timothy 3:16, 17 tells us that Scripture is useful for learning to do what is right and bringing correction to what we are doing wrong. Study passages about the home and obey what God's Word says.

Pray for Wisdom

Pray for wisdom with faith, not doubting just like it tells us to do in James 1:5. God will pour out wisdom, insight, and understanding for our task as homemakers….if we ask Him.

Training

Be trained by older, godly homemakers we are commanded in Titus 2:3-5 while Proverbs 19:20 reminds us to listen to advice and accept instruction. I want to keep growing in excellence as a homemaker. How about you?

One thing I do is watch other homemakers and pick up things that I can imitate. Sometimes I borrow recipes, traditions, or family night ideas. I also listen to other godly homemakers when they give advice. Books written by godly homemakers are another source of wisdom in my career as a homemaker.

Husband's Goals

Find out your husband's goals for the home and his personal needs/desires. Seek to serve him in those areas. Proverbs 31:11 & 12 tells us to bring our husbands good, not harm, all the days of their lives. Honor your husband. Create a home for him that is his "castle" and refuge.

Household Administration

Be organized! Have a schedule! Have a plan! A prudent wife watches carefully over the affairs of her household with diligence and vigilance. Set goals and make a plan to reach them. Make a schedule and a budget—then stick to them! De-clutter and put everything in its proper place. Organize your closet, your computer, and your life. Life is easier when you have a plan and a place to make it happen.

Psalm 90:12 tells us to number our days so that we can have a heart filled with wisdom. I am fifty years old as I write this. Now, unless I live another fifty years, my life is already half over. I realize that I am limited in how much of life I have left so I need to make sure that I accomplish all that God wants me to do.

Your children's childhood years in your home will be short. The days and years will fly by quickly. Life itself is a vapor, the wind passes over, and we are soon in the Presence of our precious Jesus. Take care to keep in mind the brevity of life so that you do not waste it.

Student

Be a student—learn all you can! Keep a notebook, file, or other easy-access way to store information. Proverbs 23:12 commands us to apply our hearts and ears to listen and learn. As we take homemaking seriously, we want to grow in our calling like a disciple, or student.

The First Artist/What is Hidden Art?

Homemaking is preparing and maintaining a home for those you love. It is a ministry unto the Lord and a service for your family. What a great privilege it is to create a home!

Read *The Hidden Art of Homemaking*, Chapter #1

What is homemaking?

_____

_____

_____

_____

_____

_____

How is art involved in homemaking?

_____

_____

_____

_____

_____

_____

Homemaking is preparing and maintaining a home for those you love.

Let's compare homemaking to a person's physical body. We have the frame of homemaking and the form of homemaking. The frame is like the skeleton and the form is like the muscle and skin.

Frame (skeleton): cleaning, time management, budgeting, rules, discipline, diet, nutrition.

Form (muscle, skin, etc.): relationships, art, life!, joy, godly children who love Jesus!

The frame is the means to the end—a lovely form. Without the frame, we would be saggy, baggy, sloppy, and unable to accomplish anything. Without the outer form, homemaking is drudgery and just an endless cycle of laundry, cooking and cleaning. Who wants that?

So we add beauty to homemaking, but beauty is birthed in order. Art is beautiful. Art is birthed in order. Clutter, debt, and lack of discipline are all oppressive, stifling creativity.

As we talk about the artistic side of homemaking—be sure to schedule it in, budget for it, and prepare an orderly home to receive it.

What is art?

_____
_____
_____
_____
_____

What is an artist?

_____
_____
_____
_____
_____

Put Together a Sewing Kit

Put together a sewing kit to use this year.

You will need a small basket with a lid, a plastic box with a lid, or a sewing basket from a fabric store. Make sure the lid stays shut so younger brothers and sisters don't get into it. They might cut themselves on pins or scissors.

Here are the things you will need to put in the sewing kit:

- Good Pair of Sewing Scissors
- Tape Measure
- Straight Pins
- Pin Cushion
- Hand Needles & Sewing Needles
- White, Black, & Various Colors Spools of Thread
- Bobbins
- Seam Ripper
- Fray Check

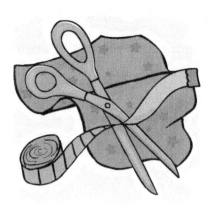

Week Two Meet with Mom

Recite Proverbs 31.

Discuss *Jesus, Fill My Heart & Home*

- Describe a spiritual makeover.
- What kind of spiritual makeover do you need?

Discuss *Hidden Art of Homemaking*

- Define Hidden Art.
- Why is Hidden Art valuable to God, and to us?

Sew a Pillowcase

Make a Standard Pillowcase

Supplies

> 1 Yard Cotton Fabric
>
> Matching Thread
>
> 1 Dozen Straight Pins

Tools

> Sewing Machine
>
> Iron
>
> Scissors
>
> Tape Measure
>
> Ruler

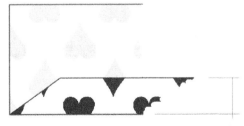

Wash, dry, and iron flat the fabric, making sure that all corners are square (90° angles.) Measure carefully and trim the fabric to be exactly 36"x42".

Using the ruler to measure, fold down, with wrong side of fabric together, 1" of 42" wide fabric. Press fold with iron.

4.00"

Using the ruler to measure, fold down this same edge, with wrong side of fabric together, 4" of 42" wide fabric. Press fold with iron.

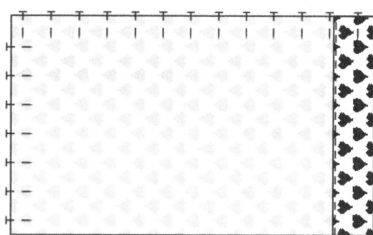

With the sewing machine set to a standard seam stitch, run a row of stitches ½" from the folded edge, back-stitching at each end.

Fold fabric in half across folded edge, with right sides together. This will leave you with a rectangle measuring 31"x21". Pin the wrong sides together of the long edge and the edge opposite the folded.

With the sewing machine set to a standard seam stitch, run a row of stitches ½" from the edge of the pinned edges, pulling out the pins before they reach the sewing machine pressure foot.

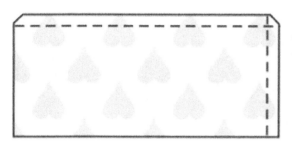

Snip off sewn corners. Fold the pillowcase right side out. Press entire pillowcase flat with hot iron.

Week Two Home

Memorize Proverbs 31:10-31

Write Proverbs 31:10-31 in the version of your choice. I recommend NASB or NKJ or ESV. Then say the passage aloud.

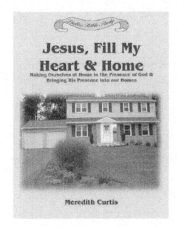

Jesus, Fill My Heart & Home Lesson 2

"Make Ourselves at Home in the Presence of God through Abiding in His Word"

Read and Answer Questions

What is Hidden Art?

Read *The Hidden Art of Homemaking*, Chapter #2

Homemaking is preparing and maintaining a home for those you love. It is a ministry unto the Lord and a service for your family. What a great privilege it is to create a home!

How does God display His ability as an artist? What is His artwork?

_____

_____

_____

_____

_____

_____

_____

_____

"God saw all that He had made, and it was very good. And there was evening and morning---the sixth day" (Genesis 1:31 NIV ©1979).

"Now the LORD God had planted a garden in the east, in Eden; and there he put the man He had formed" (Genesis 2:8 NIV ©1979).

You can see two things. The first is that God created many things in six days and everything was good. The second thing you see is that God arranged his artwork. He planted a garden, arranging the flowers, and placed another piece of artwork there: man. Eden was like an art show.

"The heavens declare the glory of God; the skies proclaim the work of his hands. Day after day they pour forth speech; night after night they display knowledge. There is no speech or language where their voice is not heard. Their voice goes out into all the earth, their words to the ends of the world" (Psalm 19:1-4 NIV ©1979).

What does this psalm teach us about God's creation, the skies?

_____

_____

_____

_____

_____

_____

"The wrath of God is being revealed from heaven against all the godlessness and wickedness of men who suppress the truth by their wickedness, since what may be known about God is plain to them, because God has made it plain to them. For since the creation of the world God's invisible qualities—His eternal power and divine nature—have been clearly seen, being understood from what has been made, so that men are without excuse," (Romans 1:18-20 NIV).

What do we learn about God's artwork (Creation) here?

_____

_____

_____

_____

_____

_____

How can creation reveal God's power and divine nature?

_____

_____

_____

_____

_____

_____

Here are some principles of art from a Christian perspective.

- Art is created by a person (God is a Person!)
- Art reveals that character and personality of the artist (Creation reveals God!)
- Art is set in place, put somewhere or put to some use: displayed!
- Art is given to self or others to enjoy and appreciate; beyond functional! (God saw that what He made was good!)
- A Christian above all others should live creatively, artistically and aesthetically.

Define the following words.

Creativity:

_____

_____

_____

_____

Artistic:

_____

_____

_____

_____

Aesthetic:

_____

_____

_____

_____

Creativity demonstrates that we are made in the image of God. Homemaking is full of opportunities to be creative.

Andrea and I were both young moms with two small daughters and not much money. But, Andrea had the prettiest home I have ever seen. She found bargains everywhere and worked magic with her sewing machine making curtain, ruffles, wall hangings, and wall coverings. Her creativity was beautiful. What a lovely home!

Read _Hidden Art of Homemaking_ page 212 about missionaries' lack of beauty in their home turning these Africans away from Gospel. Have you ever worried that making something beautiful or spending a little money to add loveliness to your home is a waste of money? Well, I'm not advocating extravagance, but please feel free to create a lovely home for your family. Look at the beautiful world God created for use to enjoy. We are made in the image of God.

"Then God said, "Let us make man in our image, in our likeness, and let them rule over the fish of the sea and the birds of the air, over the livestock, over all the earth, and over all the creatures that move along the ground."

"So God created man in His own image, in the image of God He created him; male and female He created them. God blessed them and said to them, "Be fruitful and increase in number; fill the earth and subdue it. Rule over the fish of the sea and the birds of the air and over every living creature that moves on the ground."

"Then God said, "I give you every seed-bearing plant on the face of the whole earth and every tree that has fruit with seed in it. They will be yours for food. And to all the beasts of the earth and all the birds of the air and all the creatures that move on the ground—everything that has the breathe of life in it—I give every green plant for food." And it was so.

"Thus the heaven and earth were completed in their vast array.

"By the seventh day God had finished the work he had been doing; so on the seventh day he rested from all his work. And God blessed the seventh day and made it holy, because on it He rested from all the work of creating that He had done" (Genesis 1:26-2:3 NIV ©1979).

We are made in God's image. What does that mean?

_____
_____
_____
_____

If God is a creative artist, what does that make us?

_____

We are God's artwork! We are also his artists in training.

"For you created my inmost being; you knit me together in my mother's womb. I praise you because I am fearfully and wonderfully made; your works are wonderful, I know that full well. My frame was not hidden from you when I was made in the secret place. When I was woven together in the depths of the earth, your eyes saw my unformed body. All the days ordained for me were written in your book before one of them came to be" (Psalm 139:13-16 NIV ©1979).

"For we are God's workmanship, created in Christ Jesus to do good works, which God prepared in advance for us to do," (Ephesians 2:10 NIV).

"....being confident of this, that He who began a good work in you will carry it on to completion until the day of Christ Jesus" (Philippians 1:6 NIV ©1979).

We are beloved!

"Be imitators of God, therefore, as dearly loved children" (Ephesians 5:1 NIV©1979).

Who is commanded to imitate God?

_____
_____

Why doesn't He address us as "children who dearly love God" instead of "dearly loved children"?

_____
_____
_____
_____

"How great is the love the Father has lavished on us, that we should be called children of God. And that is what we are! The reason the world does not know us is that it did not know Him. Dear friends, now we are children of God and what we will be has not yet been made known. But we know that when He appears, we shall be like him, for we shall see Him as He is" (I John 3:1-2 NIV ©1979).

What evidence do we have that God loves us?

_____
_____
_____
_____

What is the amount of love God has for us?

_____
_____

What two things will happen when Jesus appears?

_____
_____

Remember this principle: seeing Jesus as He is leads to becoming like Him. We need time with Him, to see Him as He is by reading the Bible, praying, worshipping, and abiding in Christ.

We imitate God when we are creative and we enjoy art and beauty!

"Command those who are rich in this present world not to be arrogant nor to put their hope in wealth, which is so uncertain, but to put their hope in God, who richly provides us with everything for our enjoyment" (I Timothy 6:17 NIV ©1979).

"The thief comes only to steal and kill and destroy; I have come that they may have life, and have it to the full" (John 10:10 NIV ©1979).

We are to be thankfully enjoying life! We start our career in homemaking with a thankful heart, grateful for God's love and beauty. Just as God created our earthly and heavenly home out of love, we will create our family's home out of love.

I love looking at homemaking in this fresh way! As homemakers we are artists-in-training. God is teaching us to create a place of beauty that will nurture the souls and spirits of our family.

Week Three Meet with Mom

Recite Proverbs 31.

Discuss *Jesus, Fill My Heart & Home*

- How you spend more time in the Word?
- How can you get more out of your time in the Word?

Discuss *Hidden Art of Homemaking*

- Describe God as an Artist.
- What are some of your favorite masterpieces created by God?

Finish Pillowcase.

Prayer Focus:

- Growing in God's Word
- Reflecting God, the First Artist

Week Three Home

Memorize Proverbs 31:10-31

Write Proverbs 31:10-31 in the version of your choice. I recommend NASB or NKJ or ESV. Then say the passage aloud.

Jesus, Fill My Heart & Home Lesson 3

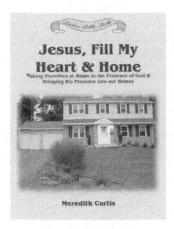

"Am I Praying Loud Enough for God to Hear Me?"

Read and Answer Questions

Music

Homemaking is preparing and maintaining a home for those you love. It is a ministry unto the Lord and a service for your family. What a great privilege it is to create a home!

Read *The Hidden Art of Homemaking*, Chapter #3

How does God display His ability as an artist/musician? What is His artwork?

_____

_____

_____

_____

_____

_____

When life becomes hectic, we often set aside our musical and artistic talents. Our family suffers from this deprivation because music and art fill our homes with beauty and joy!

Is there creativity inside you that is longing to burst out through a painting that you paint or a funny cartoon that you sketch? Is there a song inside your heart that you need to sing or play on an instrument?

Music should always be part of a family because it is a safe, fun, and festive way to express your heart. Music brings a depth to emotion.

You can also listen to music and discuss music. You do not have to be a great musician to enjoy music. But don't limit yourself either. Maybe there is a singer or musician wanting to come out. Whether you are talented or not, make a joyful noise for the Lord. ☺

This chapter encourages us to listen to variety of good music. Some of us need to stretch our musical tastes. Sing and dance with your husband and children. What joyful times I've had singing and dancing around the living room with my little ones.

"Praise the LORD. Sing to the LORD a new song, his praise in the assembly of the saints. Let Israel rejoice in their Maker; let the people of Zion be glad in their King. Let them praise His name with dancing and make music to Him on the tambourine and harp. For the LORD takes delight in His people; He crowns the humble with salvation. Let the saints rejoice in this honor and sing for joy on their beds. May the praise of God be in their mouths" (Psalm 149:1-6a NIV ©1979).

Where are the different places that people are encouraged to worship the Lord with music?

_____

_____

_____

_____

Which are private?

_____

_____

_____

_____

Which are public?

_____

_____

_____

_____

Name all the different musical expressions we are encouraged to do?

_____

_____

_____

_____

"Praise the LORD. Praise God in His sanctuary; praise Him in His mighty heavens. Praise Him for His acts of power; praise Him for His surpassing greatness. Praise Him with the sounding of the trumpet, praise Him with the harp and lyre, praise him with tambourines and dancing, praise him with the strings and flute, praise him with the clash of cymbals, praise him with resounding cymbals. Let everything that has breath praise the LORD. Praise the LORD" (Psalm 150:1-6 NIV ©1979).

Name all the different instruments God wants to hear praising Him.

_____

_____

_____

_____

"Let the peace of Christ rule in your hearts, since as members of one body you were called to peace. And be thankful. Let the word of Christ dwell in you richly as you teach and admonish one another with all wisdom, and as you sing psalms, hymns and spiritual songs with gratitude in your hearts to God" (Colossians 3:15-16 NIV ©1979).

What are the three prerequisites to teaching others and singing to God?

_____

_____

_____

_____

When peace rules in our hearts, we are drawn to one another in unity. Remember we are living stones being built together as a temple. The Lord also mentions thankfulness. Thanking God leads right into praising Him with a song! The Word of God can dwell in us richly by reading, studying, and meditating on the Word of God. When the Word of God dwells in us richly, it should always lead to obedience and worship.

"Do not be drunk on wine which leads to debauchery. Instead, be filled with the Spirit. Speak to one another with psalms, hymns and spiritual songs. Sing and make music in your heart to the Lord, always giving thanks to God the Father for everything, in the name of our Lord Jesus Christ" (Ephesians 5:18-20 NIV ©1979).

What is the counterfeit to being filled with the Holy Spirit?

_____

How is praise and worship public?

_____

_____

_____

How is praise and worship private?

_____

_____

_____

When we worship, we should focus our mind on Jesus. We can train our children when they are young to think about Jesus when they sing Him songs.

Make a Family Worship Songbook

This week you will make a family worship songbook for everyone to use to worship the Lord together.

Here are the directions.

- Choose your songs. They should include songs that everyone likes or at least one favorite song per person, in addition to songs you like.
- Type the lyrics up. If anyone plays the guitar or piano, add chords so he or she can play while you sing.
- Print the lyrics on 3-hole punch paper (or print and use a 3-hole puncher)
- Place the printed songs inside a folder with 3 prongs, choosing the color of your choice.
- Make a beautiful songbook cover and glue it to the front of the folder.

Take a picture of your songbook and glue the photo in the box below.

My Songbook

Casseroles: A Whole Meal in 1 Dish

Casseroles are the ultimate comfort food. An entire meal is baked together and served. Sometimes, you can make casseroles ahead and freeze them.

They are easy to make with just a few ingredients tossed together and baked in the oven.

They are delicious to eat. Family favorites are often these simple-to-make casseroles.

Here is a simple formula for making casseroles:

1 main ingredient (usually meat or protein) + 1 or more vegetables $_+$ starch + 1 binder (with milk or another liquid to make it creamy) + 1 topping.

Here are some suggestions for the formula. Try mixing and matching them for a unique casserole. Add some suggestions at the bottom of the chart.

Meat or Protein	Vegetable	Starch	Binder	Topping
Ground Beef, browned and drained	Beans	Pasta	Mushroom Soup	Shredded Cheese
Cooked Cubed Chicken	Carrots	Potatoes	Cream of Chicken Soup	Breadcrumbs
Canned Tuna	Onions & Green Peppers	Brown Rice	White Sauce	Crushed Potato Chips
Sausage, browned and chopped	Green Beans	White Rice	Cheese Sauce	Crushed Ritz Crackers
Ham, chopped	Mixed Vegetables	Quinoa	Sour Cream	Crushed Tortilla Chips
Steak, chopped	Broccoli	Barley	Cream of Celery Soup	Toasted Slivered Almonds
Shrimp	Scallions	Yellow Rice	Yogurt	Croutons
Lamb	Tomatoes	Corn	Salsa	
Pork	Cucumber	Beans		

Are you ready to experiment?

Try out some casseroles using the formula and see what you come up with. If a dish turns out yummy, name it and write the recipe down. Don't forget to put it in your recipe file.

Here Are My Experiments with Casseroles

Casserole #1: _____

Ingredients: _____   _____

_____   _____

_____   _____

_____   _____

How My Family and I like It and Comments: _____
_____
_____
_____
_____
_____
_____

Casserole #2: _____

Ingredients: _____   _____

_____   _____

_____   _____

_____   _____

How My Family and I like It and Comments: _____
_____
_____
_____
_____
_____

Casserole Recipes

Here are some tried and true casserole recipes you can try.

Lasagna

½ lb. Lasagna Noodles

1 lb. Ricotta Cheese

2 lb. Spaghetti Sauce

2 Eggs

1 Cup Parmesan Cheese

Cover bottom of 8" x 11" baking dish with some sauce. Lay Noodles in rows on top to cover sauce. Blend eggs and cheese together. Spoon cheese mixture on top of noodles and spread it out evently along each noodle. Spoon sauce over the cheese. Continue to layer the ingredients until you use everything up, ending with a noodle layer. Pour a light layer of sauce on top of the final layer of noodles. Bake 350°F for 1 hour.

Spanish Rice

4 Cups White or Brown Rice, already cooked

2 Pounds Ground Beef

1 Onion, chopped

1 Green pepper, chopped

1 Can Stewed Tomatoes

1 (16 oz.) Bag Frozen Corn, thawed

Salt & Pepper to Taste

1 Tbsp. Minced Garlic

1 Tbsp. Chili Powder

Dash Hot Sauce

Dash Red Pepper

Shredded Cheddar Cheese to Cover Top

Brown beef, pepper and onion together in a cast iron frying pan. Drain off excess fat. Add in rice, tomatoes, corn, & spices. Mix thoroughly. Pour rice mixture into grease baking pan or casserole. Bake for 15 minutes. Add shredded cheese, covering the top. Bake 15 more minutes.

Shepherd's Pie

Leftover Lamb or Beef

1 Can Pea

Mashed Potatoes

Place leftover lamb or beef in a casserole. Cover with a can of peas. Top with Mashed Potatoes. Bake at 350°F for ½ hour until well heated. Serve with mint jelly.

****Keep a Ziploc® bag in the freezer for leftover meat. When you have enough (½ Cup per person) for a meal, you have an almost free meal.

Updated Shepherd's Pie

2 Pounds Ground Beef, browned & drained

1 Can Mushroom Soup

16 oz. Bag Frozen Corn

Mashed Potatoes

Shredded Cheddar Cheese

Mix ground beef, mushroom soup, and frozen corn and place in a casserole. Top with mashed potatoes & shredded cheddar cheese. Bake @ 350°F for 35 minutes.

Welcome Home: Creating Your Own Place of Beauty & Love
Book Review

By Emilie Barnes

How can you make yourself at home in your house/apartment/bedroom?

_____
_____
_____
_____
_____

What is Emilie like and what does she value? Do you feel like you got to know her as you read her book?

_____
_____
_____
_____
_____

How is her personality reflected in the pictures of her own home in the book?

_____
_____
_____
_____

How can your home give a good first impression to guests and family members?

_____
_____
_____
_____
_____
_____
_____
_____
_____
_____

How can you make the master bedroom romantic and peaceful?

_____
_____
_____
_____
_____
_____
_____

How can you make work spaces attractive?

_____
_____
_____
_____
_____
_____
_____

Share some ideas from this book that you want to try in your own home.

_____
_____
_____
_____
_____
_____
_____
_____
_____
_____
_____
_____
_____

October: Managing a Home

Memorize Proverbs 31

Jesus, Fill My Heart & Home Bible Study

Hidden Art of Homemaking

Paint

Sew an Apron

Grocery Shopping

Optional: *Managing to be Free* Book Review

(Meet with Mom weekly)

Week One Meet with Mom

Recite Proverbs 31.

Discuss *Jesus, Fill My Heart & Home*

- What things hinder your prayer life?
- How can your prayer times be more effective?

Discuss *Hidden Art of Homemaking*

- Describe God as a Musician
- How does Music bring joy to a Home?

Share Family Worship Songbooks

Prayer Focus:

- Prayer Life

Week One Home

Memorize Proverbs 31:10-31

Write Proverbs 31:10-31 in the version of your choice. I recommend NASB or NKJ or ESV. Then say the passage aloud.

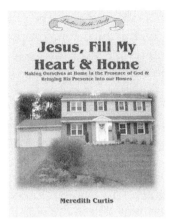

Jesus, Fill My Heart & Home Lesson 4

"Abiding in Prayer"

Read and Answer Questions

Sketching, Painting, & Sculpting

Homemaking is preparing and maintaining a home for those you love. It is a ministry unto the Lord and a service for your family. What a great privilege it is to create a home!

Read *The Hidden Art of Homemaking,* Chapter #4

How does God display His ability as an artist/painter/sculptor? What is His artwork?

_____

_____

_____

_____

_____

When we think of art, we naturally think of drawing, painting, and sculpting. Let's look for a minute at the elements of art and the principles of design. Elements of art and principles of design are the bits and pieces that form a whole greater than its individual parts. We can examine the elements of a painting or sculpture, but ultimately it is the piece as a whole that moves us emotionally.

Elements of Art

Media (plural of medium) are the materials that artists use to create art. The possibilities are endless. Art media can be watercolor paints, oil paints, sculpting with marble, sculpting with wood, paper mâché, wire, charcoals, clay, pastels, tapestry, drawing, photographs, or films.

Color is usually the first thing you notice about clothing, rooms, furniture, houses, or a piece of art. Colors come in **hues**. Red, blue, and yellow are the primary pigment colors. They are mixed to produce the secondary pigment colors: purple, green, and orange. Tertiary colors are produced by mixing primary and secondary colors. All these various colors are hues.

A color's (hue's) value is based on how light or dark it is. **Tinting** a hue simply means to add white, making it lighter. Likewise, **shading** a hue adds black to the mix, creating a darker shade. The paints you buy at Lowes to paint your house might be created from a drop of this hue, four drops of another hue, and sixteen drops of white added to the main hue. An interesting field trip to learn about pigment hues would be to visit Lowes and watch them mix paint for customers.

Red, orange, and yellow are **warm colors** exuding energy and excitement. These colors often catch your eye first in a painting. Blue, green, and purple are **cool colors** radiating peace and stillness. Cool colors often seem to fade to the background in a picture.

Lighter colors seem closer and darker colors farther away. You can create three-dimensional objects or people on a canvas by shading the sides and back, leaving the front lighter. An oval can look like a 3-D egg if the front is light and the sides are darker. Shading is an important skill in drawing—all based on the use of color!

Lines can be straight or curved; horizontal, vertical or diagonal to outline shapes (contour lines) or define the inside of a shape (interior lines). Lines can be used to create a feeling of **movement**. Curved lines create an informal, relaxed feel; straight lines create a more formal, rigid feel to a work of art. Lines can force the viewer's eye to another location in the painting.

Form or shapes are made by lines. Those basic shapes you teach your toddlers to look for around the house ("Find all the circles in the room, Tommy.") are found in art as well. Squares, circles, rectangles, and triangles make up more complicated forms.

Three dimensional art, such as sculpture, statuary, or architecture, is in their actual shape. In two dimensional art, such as paintings, shapes are formed with shading, highlighting, and the positioning of dark and light colors.

Texture can be seen or felt on the surface of any art object. Textures can be rough or smooth. They can also be implied with color and line in a painting. Oils and watercolors create a different texture on a canvas, just as wood and marble are different in a statue.

Principles of Design in Art

This is simply the way the elements of art are put together in a project. They are guidelines for a work of art.

Balance can be formal (symmetrical) or informal (asymmetrical). **Formal balance** requires both sided of the center to be alike. Even a face is not entirely symmetrical (a mole on one side or a slight turn of the nose). Formal balance, rarely used in a painting, is used in statues. **Informal balance** creates a sense of balance using size, distance, and color. A brightly colored beach ball on one side of a beach scene could balance out the palm tree on the other side (color and size). A puppy fourteen inches from the center of the tapestry could balance a grown dog very close to the center on the other side (size and distance). Two small throw pillows on one end of the couch could balance the larger pillow at the other end (size).

Dominance is the item or group of items that dominate the picture. It's what "catches your eye" when you first look at a picture! It might be large, brightly colored, unusual, or set right in the center. Sometimes the artist will "focus in" on one person or thing and allow the rest of the painting to be blurry or hazy.

Rhythm is caused by repetition or patterns. Repeating lines, shapes, or colors can form a pattern. Repetition can also be created by using different shades of the same color. Rhythm needs contrast to keep artwork from being dull.

Proportion addresses the relationship of size and shape to one another. Sizes should "match" one another and be the proper degree of size to one another. For example, an eye should be smaller than a foot, unless the face is MUCH closer than the foot. A piece of furniture should be in proportion to the rest of the furniture in the room. Even when things are bigger or brighter to provide a sense of depth, things should still "feel right."

Unity happens when texture, color, shape, rhythm, dominance, balance and proportion all work together in harmony to create an overall message or theme. These separate parts combine to form a whole. The whole art project feels like "one" not the sum of several parts.

Art Projects

You can enjoy and investigate elements of art as you look at artwork and as you create your own artwork. There are so many creative things you can enjoy together.

Almost all of art involves pattern (sketching) and filling in (oils or watercolors). Often an artist will sketch his painting first and then "color" it in.

Drawing is an essential art skill and a springboard to other arts, such as painting, calligraphy, architecture, and fashion design. Many artists and crafters use drawings as preliminaries for their future projects.

Drawing is simply making pictures with lines. Shading is added to create depth and perspective. It is the outline for a painting. Drawing strengthens hand-eye coordination and sharpens observation skills.

Although drawing and sketching can be done with pencil, ink, charcoal, and pastels, a soft pencil, soft eraser, and drawing paper are all you need to get started.

Here are some art projects you can try:

- Drawing
- Charcoal, Pastels
- Stained Glass Art
- Watercolor Painting
- Oil Painting
- Acrylic Painting
- Mixed Media Painting
- Ceramics
- Sculpture
- Stone Carving
- Photography
- Digital Imaging
- Animation, Cartooning
- Graphic Design
- Architecture
- Wire Sculpture
- Whittling
- Woodworking
- Jewelry Making
- Rubber Stamping, Embossing
- Scrapbooking
- Tole Painting
- Basket Making
- Glass Blowing
- Bead Making
- Mural
- Collage
- Miniature Scapes

Christian Artist Thomas Kinkade & His Paintings

Thomas Kinkade's artwork is loved around the world and appreciated for his use of strong contrast between darkness and light.

Thomas Kinkade has devoted his life to painting a message of faith and family values. Married to Nan since 1982, he is the father of four lovely daughters. His beautiful paintings take the viewer back to olden days where life was simpler and more virtuous.

Thomas has used his paintings to raise money for a wide variety of charities and has touched the heart of folks all over the world.

I love his style because as Christians we are filled with the light of Christ. In fact, we are commanded to "Arise and Shine" because His Light has shown upon us.

Thomas Kinkade Assignment

Go online and look at Thomas Kinkade's paintings, at least twenty of them, very carefully. Notice his use of light. You will be painting a picture that uses light like Thomas Kinkade's painting. You can use watercolor or acrylic paint to create your masterpiece.

Here is a photograph of my painting.

Grocery Shop with Mom's Weekly Grocery Money

One of the challenges for a homemaker is to provide delicious and nutritious foods, all the while, keeping to a budget.

Most homemakers have a monthly grocery budget.

Why don't you ask four different homemakers what they spend on groceries? Jot down their budgets.

_____   _____   _____   _____

Some homemakers divide the money up and spend a certain amount each month. Others, like me, do it differently. I make a large run to a warehouse store like Sam's® and stock up, using 70% of my monthly grocery budget. I use the rest to stock up on milk, bread, eggs, and other items as needed, during the rest of the month.

Shopping Assignment

Ask Mom if you can grocery shop for her this week. Make a list together and then take the money and buy the food on the list. Look for bargains, cheaper brands, and consider using coupons.

How much did you spend over or under Mom's usual budget? _____

Here's what I purchased? (Share your shopping list)

Find Your Way Around the Grocery Store

Grocery Stores are usually laid out in a similar way. The meat department is often located along the back wall. Produce is often sold on one of the side walls. On the other side, you will often find refrigerated foods and dairy.

The aisles inside contain food that doesn't have to be refrigerated. The grocery store aisles are numbered with foods listed on the signs.

Sometimes Frozen foods are located right in the middle of the store from front to back.

Go ahead and explore the grocery store. Find the following items and lists the Aisle Number next to the food.

Soft Drinks _____   Apples _____

Hot Chocolate _____   Mustard _____

Ice Cream _____   Pudding Mix _____

Steak _____   Canned Tuna _____

Once you are familiar with your grocery store, you can focus on being a wise consumer.

Unit Pricing

Unit pricing helps you figure out which item is the best buy. Unit pricing is the cost per unit of weight or measurement.

Pretend you need tomatoes. You pick up one can that weighs 16 ounces and costs 98 cents. The other can is 14 ounces and costs 90 cents.

One can is cheaper and one can is bigger. How do you find the unit price of both cans?

For the first can: $98 \div 16 = 6.0$ cents. The unit price is 6.0 cents.

For the second can $90 \div 14 = 6.43$. The unit price is 6.43 cents.

I am happy to tell you, but you don't have to bring your calculator to the grocery store. You can find the unit price on the label, along with the price and weight.

Compare two cans of refried beans at the grocery store.

Can #1 _____

    Price _____   Unit Price _____   Weight _____

Can #2 _____

    Price _____   Unit Price _____   Weight _____

Which can of refried beans is the better buy? _____

Compare two cans of baking powder at the grocery store.

Can #1 _____

    Price _____   Unit Price _____   Weight _____

Can #2 _____

    Price _____   Unit Price _____   Weight _____

Which can of baking powder is the better buy? _____

Compare two jars of salsa at the grocery store.

Jar #1 _____

    Price _____   Unit Price _____   Weight _____

Jar #2 _____

    Price _____   Unit Price _____   Weight _____

Which jar of salsa is the better buy? _____

Week Two Meet with Mom

Recite Proverbs 31.

Discuss *Jesus, Fill My Heart & Home*

- Discuss abiding prayer and how to walk in them more and more.
- How can your prayer times be more effective right now and in the future as a homemaker?

Discuss *Hidden Art of Homemaking*

- Describe God as a Painter/Sculptor.
- How does God use color, form, texture, line, and unity in creation?
- What are your favorite Masterpieces that God has created with color, line, form, texture, and unity?

Share Shopping with Mom's Grocery Money Experience.

Paint a House Thomas Kinkade Style with Light shining through the windows. Use watercolor or acrylic. Make sure that you protect your clothing and your painting space. If you have already painted them, share your paintings.

Prayer Focus:

- Worship together.

Week Two Home

Memorize Proverbs 31:10-31

Write Proverbs 31:10-31 in the version of your choice. I recommend NASB or NKJ or ESV. Then say the passage aloud.

Jesus, Fill My Heart & Home Lesson 5

"Walking & Dancing with Jesus"

Read and Answer Questions

Family Finances & the Economic Cycle

A healthy economy goes up and down in a cycle. There are times of economic growth and times of economic down-turns, or recessions.

Think of your own life as an example. There are seasons of spending and seasons of saving.

Seasons of spending include buying back-to-school supplies, purchasing Christmas presents, paying for a family vacation, or acquiring a brand-new computer. In all those situations, you are putting money into the economy, helping the economy grow.

Seasons of saving include saving for the family vacation, putting money aside for Christmas gifts, or pinching pennies to put extra aside for a brand new computer.

You get the picture. If you are spending money all the time, there will be no money saved up. If you need to buy something, you will have to go into debt if you do not have savings.

A healthy economy is not always growing, rather it goes through cycles of growing and recessing. This normal cycle is the result of many things, including the need for businesses and people to save money for seasons of spending. Before we look at the stages of a normal economic cycle, let's look at the factors that determine each stage.

In the Garden of Eden, Adam had a job, but it was an easy work—taking care of the garden and the animals. There was plenty to eat, a rent-free place to live, and wholesome fun to participate in for free. They didn't even have to water the plants. A mist came up out of the ground. Since the fruit-incident, mankind must get a job and work hard to take care of needs (food, clothing, shelter) and wants (cars, phones, vacations, computers).

Over time, people have made things to sell to other people to make money to buy the things their own families need. Other people provide services to bring a paycheck home that will buy necessities. All this buying and selling, the flow of money, the cost of goods and services, and how much stuff is actually produced is called the economy. This economy ebbs and flows: expanding, booming, contracting, recessing, and recovering—the economic cycle.

The economy involves a wide variety of people all over the world who work hard to provide products for people to buy. When lots of people buy their products, the producers will make money so they can provide for their families. Let's look at the natural rhythm of the economy called the economic cycle.

For someone to make something to sell, he/she must look around and gather available resources (cloth, oranges). To this is added hard work. Polly turns cloth into clothing with sewing (work). Jennifer picks and boxes (work!) oranges to ship to customers in another state.

The stages in an economic cycle are Expansion, Prosperity, Contraction, Recession, and Recovery. We will look at business owners Polly, Jennifer, and Jim.

Expansion

This is a season of growing and increasing in productivity. Often business owners will increase their efficiency which, in turn, increases productivity and profit. When this is happening to many businesses at the same time, consumers start buying more stuff at cheaper prices (due to increased efficiency!)

Jennifer expands her orange shipping business by hiring more people to pack oranges in boxes to ship. She adds to her customer base too. The profits begin to grow more and more each month. Jennifer is experiencing expansion in her business.

Prosperity

Affluence, wealth, and good cheer are in abundance in a season of prosperity. Businesses are bringing in profits and using these profits to expand their companies or start new ones. Some Christian businessmen use times like this in their business to help young men start their own businesses. Stock prices are usually high because businesses are prospering.

Jennifer purchases another orange grove debt-free when she moves from a period of expansion to one of prosperity. As the profits pour in, she is careful to tithe, save, increase her employees' pay, and purchases some needed equipment. This is a wise use of the season of prosperity. Some people are not wise during prosperity and spend all their money.

Contraction

This is a period of economic decline for a business. Prices drop. Sales slow down, people are buying less, and families start tightening their belts. This is a time where unsuccessful businesses must make hard decisions. Inefficient business practices must change or the business could fold. Marketing practices are analyzed. New ways to improve the product are discovered.

Polly's business is struggling. She has to let two of her employees go. She gives them six months notice and allows them one day a week to look for another job. She finds a cheaper place to purchase zippers and buttons, freeing up some money to fix two of her sewing machines. She asks her employees to help her come up with improvements that will make her clothing more marketable. One of her seamstresses has an advertising plan that becomes very popular. Sales increase and she hires back the employees she had to let go. Polly made wise use of her season of contraction. When finances get tight, don't get scared. Pray and ask God for wisdom to make smart decisions.

Recession

A recession is similar to a contraction, but felt more strongly by more of the population. In a recession, production slows down, profits decrease, and consumer spending decreases. People are making less money, losing their jobs, or afraid of losing their jobs, so they spend less money. Unemployment rates begin to rise. Interest rates often go up or banks are less willing to lend money across the board, not just to high-risk borrowers. Even during a recession, God provides for His people.

Recovery

During recovery, things begin to improve. People start back to work who were unemployed, production increases, sales increase. Recovery is similar to expansion, but feels different because often people have to "catch up" financially.

Jim and his family could not go to the dentist or buy clothes during the recession. Now that Jim's bicycle business is up and running, they have to catch up on purchases that were put off until later. Any extra money goes to buying shoes, clothing, and paying the dentist. Once they are back on their feet, the recovery season will feel like a season of expansion again.

Recovery is the time to get back on track financially, hopefully with more wisdom and take care of any needs from the recession.

How Cycles Help

We all love seasons of expansion and prosperity. It is fun when money is rolling in, but often these seasons cause prices to jump up to unreasonable places. A season of contraction will bring those prices back down to a more reasonable level.

If we, as Christians want to avoid debt, then we need to tighten our belts and save once in a while. We also need seasons that force us to examine our business practices, expenses, and policies. It often takes lean times to bring out creative ideas. After all, necessity is the mother of invention.

As Christians, we know that God's promises hold true in every season of the economic cycle, even when the government is intervening to help and causes more harm than good. Our provider is not hindered by economic down-turns. He owns the cattle on a thousand hills. He is able to provide in season and out of season. We are always blessed!

How Economics Affects Our Personal Lives

Economic cycles don't just affect nations and leaders, they affect families and individuals.

Economic principles can help you to prosper as a family. Understanding how debt works will help you avoid it, along with learning biblical principles. You will need to make changes in your family finances depending on what is happening in the economy at large.

You will also need to pay attention to your family economic cycle. When times are good, make sure to save money instead of spending it freely. If expensive things loom ahead (weddings, college, new car), you need to start saving years ahead. When times are tight, prayerfully cut expenses and streamline your spending.

Grocery Shop with ½ Mom's Weekly Grocery Money

In your own household in the future, you will experience different components of the economic cycle. Sometimes money will be flowing and other times, things will be tight financially. We are going to learn how to deal with lean times by shopping with only half of Mom's grocery budget this week. When times are tough, you will have to cut expenses. Often, that affects the grocery budget.

You will have to make a plan this week to feed your family on half the money. Have fun!

Shopping Assignment

Ask Mom if you can grocery shop for her this week. Make a list together and then take the money and buy the food on the list. Look for bargains, cheaper brands, and consider using coupons. Remember you only have half of the usual amount.

How much did you spend over or under Mom's usual budget? _____

Here's what I purchased? (share your shopping list)

_____ _____ _____

_____ _____ _____

_____ _____ _____

_____ _____ _____

_____ _____ _____

_____ _____ _____

_____ _____ _____

_____ _____ _____

_____ _____ _____

8 Secrets Every Homemaker Should Know

Successful homemakers have acquired wisdom that comes from years of on-the-job training.

Loving your husband, raising children, and managing a home is not a job for the faint-hearted. Here are some secrets to help you experience joy and success in your homemaking adventure.

Secret #1: Patterns & Habits

Set up patterns and habits in your home to instill security and create a restful environment. Daily, weekly, and yearly routines allow family members to fall into peaceful patterns of living.

Annual customs such as holidays, birthdays, vacations, and seasonal activities come along each year, giving everyone in the family things to look forward to.

Weekly habits such as attending church on Sunday mornings, taking part in Bible study on Wednesdays, enjoying family night on Friday, doing laundry on Thursdays, and cleaning together on Saturday morning gives the household a rhythm to each week that is predictable.

Daily routines such as mealtimes, schooling hours, chore time, and daily devotions repeated over and over again produce a sense of order and peace in any home. Nighttime and morning routines are especially important. Our children were raised to do their "five things" when they woke up each morning: brush teeth, get dressed, make bed, have a Quiet Time, and clean room. Each evening, Mike read a bedtime story to the children and prayed over them before tucking them in at night.

Secret #2: Realistic Expectations

Each member of a household should have realistic expectations of themselves and one another. Keeping an immaculate home with a toddler underfoot is possible, but not necessarily a noble goal.

You will have horrible days and terrific days. Don't expect to enjoy every single day of homemaking. No one I know enjoys their job every single day.

Children blow it, make a mess, and embarrass you. So do husbands. Oh, and you will not be perfect either. Set your heart on Jesus–He is the only one who is perfect. His love will overshadow the imperfections of yourself and others.

Secret #3: Keep the Main Things the Main Things

It is easy to get distracted and focus on unimportant tasks, neglecting the eternal ones. Your main job is to support your husband, train your children in the way God wants them to go, and create a home that is warm and welcoming.

If your home decorating project keeps you from spending time each day reading aloud to your children, then you are getting distracted by the less important things.

With that said, there are so many creative ways you can make your home a beautiful, celebrate joyfully, and stir up a love of learning.

Secret #4: Get Rid of Everything that Isn't Useful or Beautiful

Pare down to things that are useful to make life easier or add beauty to your home. Books, of course, are always useful. Good music, pots, pans, a globe, lamps, and desks are all examples of useful items. In addition, we want to be surrounded by beauty. Paintings, photographs, area rugs, throw pillows, and plaques may not be useful, but if they are beautiful, they are worth their weight in gold.

You might consider getting rid of broken furniture, ripped clothing, ugly things that have no usefulness, uncomfortable furniture, ripped linens, and anything with frayed electrical cords.

Secret #5: Have a Place for Everything & Keep Everything in its Place

Make sure that clothing, food, utensils, books, DVDs, CDs, blankets, pencils, pens, pot holders, and anything else you can think of has a place to be. Straighten up regularly, returning things to their rightful place. This will keep your home tidy.

Make sure an item's place is easy to get to if you use an item often. If not, people will get it out and leave it out. That's why people put a pencil holder with pens and pencils next to the phone with a pad of paper.

Pots and pans should be kept close to the oven and coffee mugs stored close to the coffee pot. Make sure that you have a spot to plug in and charge laptops, tablets and phones.

If there's something you find created disorder over and over (like shoes or coats), ask yourself if there is a convenient place for them to be stored. If not, create one.

Secret #6: Fill Your Home with Things that Nurture

As woman, we are created to bring forth life and nurture it. That's true in our homes, too. Fill your home with things that nurture your family spiritually, physically, emotionally, and intellectually.

Store Bibles and inspirational books on an easily-accessible bookshelf so it's easy for family members and guests to grab one whenever they need it. Fill the kitchen with nutritious food and snacks.

Create an atmosphere that communicates to each family member that they are special. Bedrooms are a great place to personalize for children. When my son turned twelve, we got rid of his cute train bedspread (which he covered with a blanket) and got a new bedspread, curtains, and wall hanging with the theme of his favorite football team: Philadelphia Eagles. Mike also painted a portion of one wall with chalkboard paint so he can write on his wall. This communicated value to our son. Now, if I had fixed Jenny Rose's room up the same way, it would not have communicated the same message.

Fill your home with maps, books, globes, good music, instruments, paint, art paper, and craft supplies to encourage intellectual growth and creativity. Let your kids bake, cook, and experiment in the kitchen.

Secret #7: Focus on the Positive

Life is full of ups and downs, but we can choose what we focus on. Cultivate gratefulness and focus on the bright side of things. This will create a joyful atmosphere in your home.

You've heard the old saying, "If Momma ain't happy, aint nobody happy." While I don't appreciate the poor grammar, I do agree with the sentiment. As homemakers, we create the atmosphere in our home.

If we are lighthearted, kind, and thoughtful, people will love being in our home because the atmosphere is one of acceptance and joy.

Laughing, joking, and silliness lighten up a gloomy atmosphere quickly. There's always something funny going on; you just have to keep your eyes open. Jokes, as long as they are not sarcastic or put-downs, can get the whole family laughing.

Affection is another atmosphere builder. Greet one another each morning with a cheery hello and a hug. Kiss or hug each other goodbye before anyone leaves the house. Greet family members when they come home, especially Daddy. Stop what you are doing and greet guests when they stop in.

Secret #8: Love

Love is what everyone wants and needs. Do everything you can to maintain family unity, including walking through conflict with one another and forgiving as often as necessary.

Conflict is inevitable, but disunity and division can be banned from your home. Refuse to allow anger and bitterness to fester. Read Matthew 18 about working through conflict and forgiveness. When something happens, have the people involved try to walk through it alone. If they are unable to resolve the issue, bring in one parent. Forgive one another quickly. Forgiveness is not excusing someone's behavior, but rather cancelling the debt.

Anger and yelling creates insecurity. Ban angry words from your house. Speak gently to one another and require everyone to do the same.

Affirm and encourage one another. Love one another deeply. Let your home be a safe, secure, and loving place.

Week Three Meet with Mom

Recite Proverbs 31.

Discuss *Jesus, Fill My Heart & Home*

- What role does worship play in Abiding in Jesus.
- How can you add worship to your life?

Share Shopping with ½ Mom's Grocery Money Experience. What did you learn?

Sew an apron.

Prayer Focus:

- Worship together.

Make a Short Apron

Supplies:

- 1 Yard Cotton Fabric
- 1 Yard Matching Cotton Fabric
- 1 Spool Matching Thread
- 1 Dozen Straight Pins

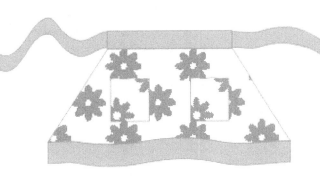

Tools:

- Sewing Machine
- Iron
- Scissors
- Tape Measure
- Ruler

Wash, dry, and iron flat the fabric. Measure carefully and cut fabric #1 into one rectangle, 36" wide and 14" tall (Piece A), and two small rectangles, 6" wide and 7.5" tall (Piece B). Cut fabric #2 into one rectangle 36" wide and 7" tall (Piece C), one rectangle 19" wide and 5" tall (Piece D), and two rectangles 23" wide and 5" tall (Piece E).

Fold the left and right edges of Piece A over ¼" from the edge of the fabric, press flat with a hot iron. Repeat these folds and press flat again. Using the sewing machine set for a top stitch, run a row of stitches ⅛" from the outside edge of these folds (and Piece A).

Fold down the top and bottom edges of Piece C ¼", wrong sides together. Press the folds flat. Fold the entire piece in half lengthwise with right sides together, making sure that the edges are perfectly lined up. Using the sewing machine set for a seam stitch, run a row of stitches along the left and right

sides. Clip off the corners of the folded end of each row of stitches. Turn Piece C right side out. With a hot iron, press flat.

Place one length of Piece C on each side of the bottom of Piece A. Pin Piece C to the bottom of Piece A, overlapping Piece A by ½" inch. Using the sewing machine set for a top stitch, run a row of stitches ⅛" from the top edge of Piece C.

Fold down all four sides of Pieces B ¼", wrong sides together. Press with hot iron. Fold down top edges of both Pieces B 1" and press the crease flat with a hot iron. These are the pockets.

Pin the wrong side of one pocket to the right side of the Piece A. Place the top right corner 6" below the top edge and 6" from the right edge. Smooth the pocket down along Piece A measuring to make sure that the entire side of this pocket is 6" from the right edge. Repeat this for the left pocket placing the top left corner 6" from the top edge and 6" from the left edge of Piece A.

Using a sewing machine set for a top stitch, run a row of stitches ⅛" from the edges of the pockets. Start about ½" from the top right corner and backstitch to the top edge. Stitch along the right side. When you reach ⅛" from the bottom of the right side turn the sewing machine knob so that the needle is buried in the fabric at the corner. Lift the feed dog and pivot Piece A to line up along the bottom of the pocket. Lower the feed dog and continue stitching. When you reach the bottom left corner repeat the same pivoting process and run a row of stitches up the left side. Backstitch at the top of this row to lock in the stitches. Repeat this process for the other pocket.

Fold down the top and bottom edges of both Pieces E, wrong sides together. With a hot iron, press the folds flat. Repeat these folds and press flat again. Using the sewing machine set for a top stitch, run a row of stitches ⅛" from the edge. Fold down opposite ends of each Piece E, ¼", with wrong sides together. With a hot iron, press the folds flat.

Fold down the top corner, wrong sides together, until the folded edge lines up perfectly with the bottom edge of Piece E. Pin in place and press the fold flat. With the sewing machine set for a top stitch, run a row of stitches ⅛" from the edge, overlapping previous seam.

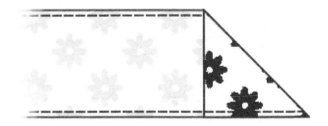

Fold two pleats in the un-sewn ends of Pieces E so that the width of each measures 2". With a hot iron, press the pleats flat. These will be the ties for the apron.

Fold down the top and bottom edges of Piece D, wrong sides together. With a hot iron press the folds flat. Fold the entire piece in half lengthwise with wrong sides together, making sure that the edges are perfectly lined up. Press this fold flat.

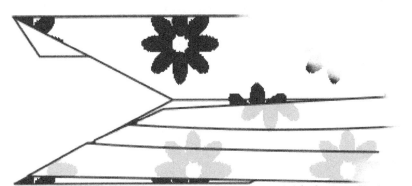

Open up the center fold of Piece D and pin one pleated end of Piece E to each end of Piece D, right sides together. Make sure that both are pinned on the same side of the center crease. Using the sewing machine set for a seam stitch, run a row of stitches ⅛" from the edge of both ties. Fold both sides in ¼" towards the center of the folded Piece D (apron ties out). Press these folds in place with hot iron.

Using the sewing machine set for a long basting stitch run two parallel lines (about ⅛" apart) ¼" from the top edge of Piece A, leaving long threads at each end of these rows of stitches. Hold on to the top threads from one side of these rows while pulling the fabric away from your hand and gathering it slightly until the gathered fabric is 18" wide. Even out ruffles across the width of the fabric.

Place one length of Piece D on each side of the top of Piece A. Pin Piece D to the top of Piece A, overlapping Piece A by ½" inch. Using the sewing machine set for a top stitch, run a row of stitches ⅛" from the edges of Piece D. Start at the top of one end, turn and run across the bottom, then turn and run up the other end.

Week Three Home

Memorize Proverbs 31:10-31

Write Proverbs 31:10-31 in the version of your choice. I recommend NASB or NKJ or ESV. Then say the passage aloud.

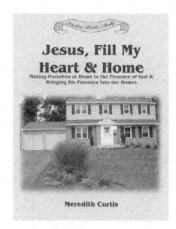

Jesus, Fill My Heart & Home Lesson 6

"Abiding in His Spirit"

Read and Answer Questions

How to Do Laundry: Sort, Remove Stains, Wash, Dry, Fold, Put Away

Laundry can seem to be never-ending in a large family.

Laundry is a big part of housekeeping if you have a large family. It can feel like your washing machine is always running. What is involved in doing the laundry? It is a simple process really. You must prepare, sort, wash, dry, fold, and put away.

Sorting Principles

If you don't sort properly, you might end up with lint, gray whites, faded colors, and ruined clothing. Everyone figures out their own way of sorting, but here are some principles to help you.

- Wash whites with whites, light colors with light colors, dark colors with dark colors
- Wash like fabrics together (I do knit loads separate from others because they pick up lint from towels and other fabrics)
- Wash very dirty clothes together
- Wash heavy clothes with heavy clothes, lighter clothes with lighter clothes
- Sort and wash according to the care label of clothing

Different Cycles

Washing Machines and Dryers have different cycles to meet various fabric needs. A **delicate cycle**, or **knit cycle**, uses gentle agitation and the wash time is shorter. A **permanent-press cycle** has a cool down period and doesn't remove as much water during the spin cycle to prevent wrinkles. **Regular cycles** have a vigorous wash cycle and the spin cycle extracts as much water as possible from the clothing. Dryers have a low heat setting for delicates and knits.

This is why you sort clothing when before you wash it.

Sort

You will need several laundry baskets and a large space to sort laundry. I do it in my family room, using a couch and two chairs to hold the baskets.

My son will gather all the hampers from every room and bring them down to the laundry room. From there, I sort the dirty clothes into several different loads. My method is a little complicated, so I will start with a simpler sorting method.

The most basic way to sort is into whites, lights, and brights/dark clothing. Many homemakers sort separate delicates into a separate pile.

When you mix towels and knits, you can get pilling on the knits, so I separate out my knits, too.

Some people separate out the towels, but my Nana was adamant that adding one towel to every load made the clothing fluffy.

Here are the different loads I sort my laundry into: whites, light knits, bright knits, dark knits, delicates, whites, lights, darks, heavy, and bleach. There are several heavy loads (jeans, sweatshirts, and towels, mostly).

You should pre-treat stains before washing.

Remove Stains

White you are sorting, you can treat stains, so they won't stay permanent. There are many great stain removers on the market. I use OxiClean®, Tide-To-Go Instant Stain Remover® Liquid Pen, and Greased Lightening®. My favorite stain remover is Dawn® dish soap. If you ever see blue on my shirt, it means that I spilled something and added Dawn® to get rid of the stain.

Make Your Own Stain Remover

Would you like to make your own stain remover? Here's a recipe.

Dawn® Dish Soap (blue)

Hydrogen Peroxide

Baking Soda

Airtight Container

Mix one part Dawn® with two parts hydrogen peroxide. Add 1-2 Tbsp. of Baking Soda to make a paste.

To use on stains: Drench stain with water. Use a toothbrush to add stain remover on top and bottom side of the fabric. Let it sit for at least an hour.

Pre-Wash

Let's talk about preparation first. There are several things you need to do to prepare laundry to be sorted and washed

- Read the care label of clothes so you know how they need to be sorted
- Zip all zippers
- Turn down cuffs
- Unbutton buttons
- Detach unwashable trim, fur, or bling
- Mend rips and tears (washing will make them worse)
- Turn polyester, nylon, and napped garments inside out
- Turn decorated T-shirts inside out

Wash

Hot cycles sanitize fabric, warm water is suitable for most loads, and cold water is best for bright colors. I like to use liquid soap or soap pods when I wash, but powdered is fine, too.

Make sure your loads are not too large or they won't get clean. Overloading can also cause damage to the washer.

Dry

You will want to dry wet clothing with a dryer or hanging clothing outside. I loved hanging clothing on the clothesline when I was a little girl.

Do not overload the dryer because it can damage the clothing and the dryer.

Fold & Put Away

Once clothing and linens are washed, it is best to fold them quickly. This will prevent wrinkles. At our house, we sort all the laundry and each person folds their own clothes and puts them away.

"How We Do Laundry" Chart

Every homemaker has her own methods of home management, including doing the family's laundry. Some moms do a load every day and some moms have a laundry day.

You will interview several homemakers and find out how they handle laundry in their homes. After you interview them, fill in the chart below.

Name of Homemaker	How often do you do laundry each week?	How many loads of laundry do per week?	What sorting method do you use?	How do you remove stains?	Who fold the laundry and puts it away?	Toughest laundry challenges?

Sort Laundry

This is a laundry sorting exercise.

Go to your room and search through your laundry hamper.

List each item in your hamper on the correct laundry basket.

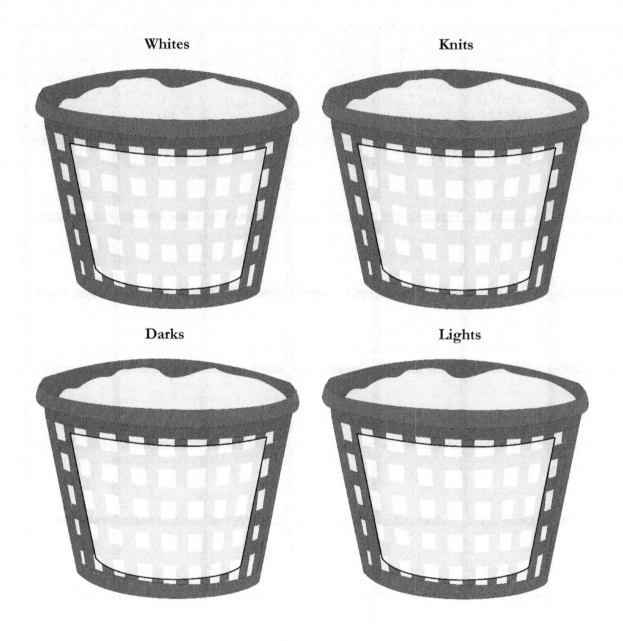

Do Family Laundry

This will be a fun assignment. You will get to do the family laundry. You will need to sort, treat stains, wash, dry, fold, and put the laundry away.

Ask Mom for any direction, input, or stipulations before you begin.

Time Management for the Homemaker

You don't clock in or out of your job as a homemaker. You will have to manage your time well to be productive and successful.

Life is so busy and there is always so much to accomplish. We make plans with the intention of devoting ourselves to good and noble purposes. But, often our good intentions are not realized because our time management skills, or lack of them, prevent us from investing the time we need to invest to fulfill our goals.

So, where do we start? How can we learn to manage our time so that we can be productive and efficient?

It starts with what we treasure.

Values

What do you value? What do you want to accomplish with your life?

Our values should be found in the Word of God. God promises us in Matthew 6:33 that is we seek His Kingdom first, He will take good care of us (my paraphrase!). We put the Lord first by making time to read His Word, pray, worship Him, spend time with His people, and share the Good News about Jesus with the lost.

If we put growing in the Lord and honoring Him with our life first in our personal life and our home school, we will experience His favor and blessing. So, keep the Lord in mind as you make your schedules and plans.

Priorities

Priorities help us to put our values into practice. My priorities are quite simple:

- God
- His People (including my family, my church family, and dear friends)
- The Lost who Need Jesus
- Everything else

This makes my life simple because my priorities revolve around relationships and serving Jesus. So, in a practical sense, spending time building relationships is more important to me than spring cleaning, though keeping my house clean and tidy is a way I can show love to my family.

What are your priorities? Always keep your priorities in mind when you are making a schedule.

Goals

Goals determine our plans and are based on our values and priorities.

"Teach us to number our days aright, that we may gain a heart of wisdom" (Psalm 90:12).

Numbering our days simply means to realize how much time we have in a day, in a year, in a life. We number our days and we realize how brief life is. There is only so much time. We must use our time wisely.

Each year, we should think about what God wants us to accomplish in the days ahead.

Plans

Plans need to be sturdy and flexible at the same time. If we number our days, we realize that there is not enough time to accomplish everything, so we will have to pick and choose based on our priorities.

If we sense the family should spend more time evangelizing, it won't just happen. We have to make a plan. Maybe we sill set aside two Sunday mornings a month to go out witnessing as a family. Or we might spend two months practicing sharing the Gospel and our testimony and then begin witnessing twice a month.

If we have a goal of getting the house organized and tidy, we could focus on one room each month.

If your goal is to give handmade Christmas presents and birthday gifts then you need to plan how you will make them. You can't make them all in December or the night before each birthday.

If my goal is to teach my child to read this year, then my plan will be to use a phonics based program so that at the end of the year, my daughter will read.

If your goal is that your child will be confident with his multiplication tables, then your plan might be to have intensive multiplication drills once a week and do multiplication reviews three times a week.

Scheduling

Plans have to be scheduled in.

If our family is going witnessing twice a month, we will have to set aside two Saturday mornings a month. If we are going to make handmade presents, we will need to devote one evening a month to the task. If we are focusing on one room each month to get the entire house tidy and organized, we will have to schedule in time to work on the monthly room.

If your plan is to use phonics to teach your child to read, when will you use the program? When will you do the reviews and drills to cultivate your child's multiplication confidence? Will it just happen? Will you do it when you "feel like it?"

If you homeschool, school plans for the year must be scheduled in. I schedule Math and Bible first thing in the morning every day. The other subjects are divided up in different time periods during the week.

Block Scheduling

I have found that rigid schedules based on hours don't work for me. I use block scheduling, based on blocks of time. I divide my days into: before breakfast, between breakfast and lunch, between lunch and dinner, and after dinner. This allows disruptions and interruptions without throwing me off my schedule. Okay, so we eat sometimes at midnight—but, hey, I'm still on my schedule.

Tools

Calendars, planners, and To-Do Lists are the most common tools we use for scheduling.

Calendars are important to have to keep track of the entire family's commitments, birthdays, and other events. A calendar should be in a highly visible place where everyone can see what's going on.

Planners can be a homemaker's best friend. I suggest using a planner with weekly schedule sheets to plan your weekly schedule.

The final thing is a To-Do List to help you stay organized and on track. On this list put specific things each day that you need to do. Don't add the things that are already on your weekly schedule (dust, cook dinner, sort laundry). Instead, add one-time things (make dentist appointment, return dress, buy airline ticket, meet college friend for dinner) to your list.

As we make our plans and commit our way to the Lord, we can look forward to a successful and joyful life and home!

A Homemaker's Schedule

I am going to give you some different scenarios and I want you to design a schedule for the following homemakers.

Rachel is a young mom with a baby, a two-year old, and a three-year old. She is nursing the baby. Rachel and her husband Thom live in a two-bedroom apartment and the children share the second bedroom. There is no dishwasher so Rachel has to wash the dishes by hand. Her husband leaves the house at 5 a.m. for work, but he is home by 3 p.m. and loves to spend time with the children so Rachel can get things done. Rachel and Thom lead a Bible study in their home on Wednesday nights, so Rachel likes to clean on Wednesdays. They go to church on Sunday mornings and eat dinner at Uncle Tad's house every Tuesday night. Rachel would really like to figure out how to get a Quiet Time in every day.

Rachel's daily chores include fixing meals, washing dishes, emptying the drainer, setting the table, clearing the table, bathing the children, dressing the children, feeding the children, playing with the children, reading to the children,

Her weekly chores include laundry, dusting, vacuuming, mopping, sweeping, ironing, cleaning the bathroom, and changing the beds.

Esther is a homeschooling mom with seven children ages 3 to 14. They live in a rambling six-bedroom farmhouse and raise chickens. The children like to sleep, but Esther wants them to get up earlier. The chores are divided between the children, but it takes everyone an hour or two each day to do chores. It takes 4 hours for the younger ones to do school and they need Esther's undivided attention. The older children finish three more hours of school during part of which the younger children nap.

Esther's daily chores include fixing meals, homeschooling the children, reading aloud to the family, and serving meals.

Esther and her family, including her husband Ron attend Rachel and Thom's Bible study and go to their church.

Lydia is the mother of four children: a six-year old, a four-year-old, a two-year old, and a baby. She is nursing the baby, teaching the six-year old to read and potty-training the two-year old. She helps her husband by doing the finances for the family business—she needs quiet to work on the finances. Lydia leads a homeschool co-op where she teaches guitar, attends Rachel and Thom's Bible study, and goes to church.

Are you ready to create schedules for each homemaker? Remember to use block scheduling.

Rachel's Schedule

Sunday	Monday	Tuesday	Wednesday	Thursday	Friday	Saturday
Breakfast	Breakfast	Breakfast	Breakfast	Breakfast	Breakfast	Breakfast
Lunch	Lunch	Lunch	Lunch	Lunch	Lunch	Lunch
Dinner	Dinner	Dinner	Dinner	Dinner	Dinner	Dinner

Esther's Schedule

Sunday	Monday	Tuesday	Wednesday	Thursday	Friday	Saturday
Breakfast	Breakfast	Breakfast	Breakfast	Breakfast	Breakfast	Breakfast
Lunch	Lunch	Lunch	Lunch	Lunch	Lunch	Lunch
Dinner	Dinner	Dinner	Dinner	Dinner	Dinner	Dinner

Lydia's Schedule

Sunday	Monday	Tuesday	Wednesday	Thursday	Friday	Saturday
Breakfast	Breakfast	Breakfast	Breakfast	Breakfast	Breakfast	Breakfast
Lunch	Lunch	Lunch	Lunch	Lunch	Lunch	Lunch
Dinner	Dinner	Dinner	Dinner	Dinner	Dinner	Dinner

Crockpot: A Meal Simmering All Day

Crockpots are wonderful! You load it up with ingredients, turn it on, and it cooks all day. Soon, there is a wonderful aroma to tantalize your taste buds all day. I love that you can leave it and forget it.

Just remember that you don't want to overfill the crockpot. You also want to keep the lid on. Finally, make sure that you defrost meat the night before so it is ready in the morning to put into the crockpot.

Here are some recipes.

You will need to make at least two crockpot meals this month. You might want to use the following recipes or find some of your own. If you really like how they turn out, add the recipes to your special recipe file box.

Overnight Coconut Oatmeal

1 ½ Cups Steel-Cut Oats

1 Can Coconut Milk

½ Cup Unsweetened Coconut

3 Tbsp. Brown Sugar

1 tsp. Vanilla

¼ tsp. Salt

4 ½ Cups Water

Brush the bottom and sides of the crockpot with melted butter. Add oats, coconut milk, water, coconut, brown sugar, vanilla, and salt. Stir until blended well. Cover and cook on low for 7-8 hours until thickened. Serve with fresh fruit.

Crockpot Chicken Stew

6 Chicken Boneless Skinless Breast Halves, or chicken parts of your choice

1 lb. Baby Carrots

2 Large Onions, chopped

5 lb. Potatoes, peel and chopped

1 Can Stewed Tomatoes

Garlic Powder, Italian Seasoning, Salt, & Pepper to Taste

1 lb. Bag Frozen Corn

1 lb. Bag Frozen Green Beans

Spray crockpot liner with non-stick cooking spray for easy clean-up. Place chicken in crockpot. Sprinkle generously with seasoning. Put onions and carrots on top of chicken. Add a layer of potatoes. Pour in stewed tomatoes. Cook on low for about 6 hours. Add frozen vegetables and cook for 2 more hours.

Lemon Herb Chicken

2-3 Pounds Chicken Boneless Skinless Chicken Breasts or Tenders

1 Lemon Cut into Wedges

2 Tbsp. Fresh Rosemary

10 Cloves Garlic

¼ Cup Chicken Broth

1 Small Pat Butter, melted

2 Pounds Small Red Potatoes, cubed

1 Pound Fresh Green Beans

Salt & Pepper to Taste

Clean chicken and pat dry. Add chicken to crockpot and drizzle with melted butter. Rub chicken with garlic. Add salt and pepper. Add garlic, broth, and potatoes. Place green beans on top of potatoes. Garnish the top of the chicken with lemon wedges. Cover. Cook on high 3-4 hours or low for 7-8 hours.

Managing to be Free: A Practical Guide to Organizing Home Priorities Book Review

By Shirley Daniels & Marian Jones Clark

Can you relate to Renae at all? In what way?

_____

_____

_____

What does it mean to set your priorities?

_____

_____

_____

What are your priorities?

_____

_____

_____

_____

_____

How can a homemaker be a thermostat instead of a thermometer?

_____

_____

_____

_____

_____

_____

What are some ways to eliminate household clutter?

_____

_____

_____

_____

Share some tips to organize the kitchen.

_____
_____
_____
_____
_____
_____
_____
_____

What is a systemized cleaning procedure?

_____
_____
_____
_____
_____
_____
_____
_____

November: Housekeeping

Memorize Proverbs 31

Jesus, Fill My Heart & Home Bible Study

Hidden Art of Homemaking

Organize, Tidy, Clean

Serge a Napkin

Interior Decorating

Optional: *Beautiful Home on a Budget* Book Review

(Meet with Mom weekly)

Week One Meet with Mom

Recite Proverbs 31.

Discuss *Jesus, Fill My Heart & Home*

- Discuss ways to experience more of the Presence of Jesus in your life.
- How will His Presence help you when you are a homemaker one day?

Discuss Laundry

- What did you learn about laundry?
- Did you have a funny experience with the laundry process?

Make Laundry Soap.

While you are making soap, discuss how scheduling & time management are important for a homemaker.

Prayer Focus:

- Wisdom for all areas of life.

Laundry Soap

1/2 Cup Borax

1 Cups Washing Soda

1 Bar Fel-Naptha Soap

3 Gallons Water

5 Gallon Bucket with Lid

Grate the entire bar of Fel-Naptha soap. (you will have a little pile of soap curls). Bring 4 Cups of the water to a boil. Bring water down to simmer. Add soap handful by handful, stirring constantly until soap is dissolved.

Pour 3 gallons into the clean five-gallon bucket. Pour in Borax, washing soda, and the pot of soap. Stir until dissolved. Put the cover on tightly. Let the mixture sit for 24 hours.

Use one cup of this laundry soap per load. Stir before you use it because it will be clumpy. Don't worry, though, the soap lumps will dissolve in the wash.

Week One Home

Memorize Proverbs 31:10-31

Write Proverbs 31:10-31 in the version of your choice. I recommend NASB or NKJ or ESV. Then say the passage aloud.

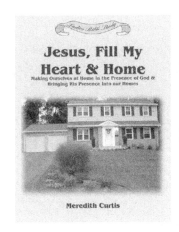

Jesus, Fill My Heart & Home Lesson 7

"Heaven, Our Real Home"

Read and Answer Questions

The Hidden Art of Cleaning

Cleaning an art?

Yes, some people are great at cleaning and organizing. A clean, tidy house makes people feel secure and safe.

When a house isn't clean and tidy, all those beautiful decorations are covered up. People are distracted by the mess and will not notice how lovely your house is.

When glass and mirrors are sparkling clean, the whole house looks prettier. When spills are wiped up off the counter and the floor is swept of debris, the kitchen is lovelier. Everywhere place in your house looks more attractive when it's clean and tidy.

Cleaning is also a matter of safety. A messy, dirty house is a breeding ground for germs, bugs, and little varmints. Food spills attract roaches and mice if not cleaned up.

If everything has a place to be and everything is in its place, it will be easy to find what you need.

How to Organize

Organizing your house is simply finding a place for everything in the house. The place should be convenient and based on how often you need to use the item. Things should be stored close to where they are used.

- Pencils and pens should be stored where people use them to write.
- Coffee cups should be stored near the coffee maker.
- Towels should be stored in or near the bathroom.
- Laundry detergent should be stored in the laundry room.

I think you get the picture. If something is difficult to get out and put away, it will most likely be left out.

I had to move my baking pans because it was difficult to stack them neatly in their location. Everyone just shoved the pans in, so when you opened the cabinet door, all the baking pans tumbled out. Now, they are in a more convenient location where putting them away and taking them out are both quite simple. That is important in our house because we bake a lot.

Where Does Everything Belong?

To organize your home, start in one room and ask yourself, "Does everything in this room have a spot where it belongs?" The next question: "Is everything's spot convenient and logical?" If the coffee cups are stored across the kitchen from the coffee maker, that's not very convenient or logical.

Now examine the storage spots themselves. Are they like the proverbial junk drawer where everything is just crammed in or is everything easy to remove and put back in.

My friend Pattie organized my kitchen junk drawer using little strawberry baskets. Now everything is easy to get ahold of.

Messy drawers and shelves can be organized using smaller baskets, bins, or containers. I like to label these containers because the rest of the family can't read my mind and know where everything is supposed to go. Labels in LARGE PRINT help everyone to put things away properly.

Group like things together for smarter storage. I put the body wash, soap, and shampoo all in one storage bin under the bathroom sink. In the kitchen, all my cooking utensils are in the same drawer. My towels and washcloths are in separate piles, but stored next to each other.

Separate and sort to make it easier to find what you are looking for. I separate my sheet set by queen, double, and twin. That way I don't have to wade through all the sheets to find one kind.

Organize books with a method that makes sense to you. I organized my living history books, biographies, and historical fiction together in order of time, from Creation to present-day. All of my songbooks are together, as well as all my anatomy books.

Organize Drawers & Closets

Life is made simple when everything has a place and everything is in its place. This is also true for dresser drawers and closets.

Socks can go in the sock draw, pajamas in the pajama drawer, and tank tops in the shirt drawer in the tank top section. The same can be done for your closet. Organizing your closet will cut down on frantic searches for clothing items.

Storage boxes and shelves in the closet can help to keep everything tidy and organized.

Give Away/Throw Away/Put Away

When you organize, you inevitably have to clean out drawers, closets, and cabinets. Make life simpler on yourself by grabbing three laundry baskets (give away, put away, and throw away) before you clean out a closet, dresser, or cabinet.

Work steadily to organize, but as you come across things you want to give away, throw away, or put away, place those items in the proper basket. One basket is for trash and things that are too damaged for anyone to use. After you are finished organized, you can throw the contents of this basket away.

How to Tidy

To tidy up is simply to put everything away in its proper place.

The best way to keep your house tidy is to follow this rule: IF YOU GET IT OUT, PUT IT AWAY! If obeyed, this rule will cut down on unnecessary clutter and make cleaning a breeze.

In our house, when it's time to tidy up, we do best if we all work together. The whole family pitches in and we work as hard and as fast as we can.

When we tidy up the family room, one person puts Rusty's toys in his toy bucket, any dirty dishes or cups to the kitchen, and gathers newspapers and throws them away. The next person starts at one end of the room and works clockwise cleaning off tabletops and making piles for each family member in the middle of the floor. The third person starts at the same place, but moves counterclockwise around the room doing the same thing. The fourth person straightens all the pillows, folds blankets, and picks up things off the floor. The fifth and sixth person start taking stuff in the piles to the correct room. The seventh person puts away any books or DVDs, straightens shelves, moves furniture back into place and runs the vacuum. And we are done!

Tidy the Bedroom

To tidy the bedroom, start by making your bed neatly and place any pillow shams, throw pillows, or blankets back on the bed. Instantly, your room will look better.

Pick up any clothes lying on the floor or furniture. Hang clean clothes up or put them in away in drawers. Put dirty clothes in the hamper. Pick up shoes and put them away in your closet.

Check drawers. Are any drawers open, even a crack? Are clothing or other items sticking out of them? Close drawers. If they won't shut, rearrange the drawers so they will shut.

Make sure there is a place for everything in your bedroom. If you read before you go to bed, there should be a place to keep your books. If you charge your phone in the bedroom, make sure you have a little docking station for it.

Start with the floor and chairs—put everything away. Next go to dresser tops—straighten and put everything away.

Keeping the Bedroom Tidy

Here are some tips to keep the bedroom tidy:

- Make your bed as soon as you wake up.
- Put clean clothes away as soon as they are washed.
- Put dirty clothes in the hamper as soon as you take them off.
- Keep a give-away bag or basket in your closet. Put any clothing or other items that you no longer need right into the bag.
- Shut all drawers and make sure they close all the way and that nothing is hanging out of them.
- Be careful of starting a "dump spot" in your bedroom when you are straightening the house. Put everything away when you straighten for company.

Tidy the Bathroom

- Start by wiping down all the sinks and counters with a damp cloth.
- Start by tossing out any trash (used tissues, ear swabs, cotton balls, dental floss, etc.) into the trash.
- Hang up all towels neatly. Put all dirty clothing into the hamper. Shake the rugs outside and straighten them. Wipe up any water on the floor.
- If your bathroom isn't organized, do that first by groups like things together (soap with shampoos, nail polishes with nail polish remover, toilet paper with tissues, extra toothbrushes with toothpaste, cosmetics together, and appliances together.
- Put everything away from the counter, except what is supposed to be there. As you tidy, throw away old cosmetics and flush medications that have expired down the toilet.
- Tidy up the tub/shower by putting everything away where it belongs. Make sure there is toilet paper on the dispenser and pick up any books or magazines from the floor. Empty the trash can.

Now that you've gone to all the trouble to tidy the bathroom, I would clean it. (See the section on

How to Clean)

Keeping the Bathroom Tidy

- Wipe down the sink after every time you use it.
- Return everything to its proper place after each use.
- Scoop up any hair from the shower floor before you exit the shower.
- Empty the trash can regularly.

Tidy the Kitchen

- Wipe out every drawer and make sure that everything is in its proper place. Unify your utensils in one drawer. Store similar things together near where they are being used. Throw out any utensils, dishes, pots, pans, glasses, or mugs that are broken.
- Wipe down every countertop and put everything away that doesn't belong out on the counter. Pick up anything on the floor and sweep. Empty the trashcan.
- As you tidy the kitchen, throw away food that is rotting or that has passed its expiration date.
- Make sure the refrigerator is organized. Move things around to their proper place. Divide the food into zones. Store food that needs to be eaten first in the front of the refrigerator.
- Organize the pantry. Get rid of any expired food. Divide the food into zones (canned good, pasta, cereal, coffee/tea, condiments, baking supplies).

Keeping the Kitchen Tidy

- Every evening put all dishes in the dishwasher or wash by hand. Clean every surface, including countertops and stove top. Sweep the floor. Empty the garbage can. This will keep the kitchen clean on a regular basis.
- As you tidy the kitchen, throw away food that is rotting or that has passed its expiration date.
- Empty the dishwasher as soon as possible after it's run.
- Swap out your dishtowel before it gets sour.
- Clean as you cook. I usually fill a sink full of hot soapy water and dump things into it as I finish using them. When I am finished cooking, I drain the water and wash the dishes. That makes less mess after dinner.

Tidy the Family Room

- Start tidying the family room by picking up and putting away all toys, books, newspapers, magazines, CDs, and DVDs.
- Straighten the cushions, blankets, and pillows. Pick up trash from the floor and tabletops.

- Close the piano and put the bench or chair underneath the piano. Pick up any dishes, cups, or glasses and take them to the kitchen.

Keeping the Family Room Tidy

Here are some tips to keep the family room tidy:

- Take dishes to kitchen whenever you finish eating or drinking
- Put away books, toys, newspaper, magazines, CDs, and DVDs when you are finished with them
- Pick up things on the floor and put them away.

How to Clean

Make the Bed

Every morning when you wake up, throw back the covers to air out the bed while you brush your teeth and wash your face. Then quickly make your bed. Just making your bed makes a difference in how your room looks. Be sure to change your sheets once a week and wash them. Every couple of months should be enough to wash your bedspread and blankets unless something spills on them.

Pull the sheets up first, making sure they are wrinkle free, and turn them over at the top about six inches. Smooth out your sheet and pull the bedspread up, making sure it is even on both sides and wrinkle-free. Pull the bedspread over the pillows and tuck a section under the pillows, make sure it is even. Lastly, put your pillow shams on top and any throw pillows used to decorate the bed.

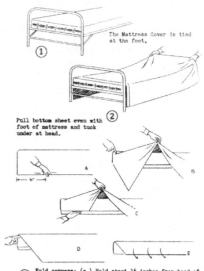

THE *Correct Way* TO MAKE YOUR BUNK

Washing Sheets & Make the Bed

Sheets and pillowcases should be changed once a week. Bedspreads, blankets, mattress pads, and pillow shams only need to be washed once a month, or even every other month.

Here is an easy way to remake your bed that is efficient and quick:

Stack bedding on a chair or tabletop in reverse order: 2 pillows, 2 pillowcases, bedspread, blanket, 2 sheets, mattress pad.

Start at the corner nearest the stack of bed linens.

Place the mattress pad over the mattress and smooth out.

Spread the bottom sheet right side up, using the center fold as a guide.

Go to the other side of the bed and tuck in the mattress pad and bottom sheet corners. If you use fitted sheets, you will need to lift the mattress a little bit to do the final corner.

Spread the top sheet right side up with the wide hem at the top, using the center fold as a guide. Go to the other side and pull the sheet smoothly, tucking the bottom in. Would you like to make hospital corners with your top sheet near the bottom of the bed? See the old guide from an United States military manual on the previous page.

Spread the bedspread over the bed, making sure it's even on each side. Fold the spread over at the top of the bed. The fold should be large enough to go over the pillows.

Place each pillow in its pillowcase. Put pillows on the bed and cover them with the bedspread.

Dust

Dust furniture often using a clean, soft cloth. Find out what furniture needs furniture polish and what needs just a dry cloth. Our dining room table requires lemon oil.

Start at one place in a room and move around the room. Make sure you dust corners and grooves. Take everything off all the tabletops and dust. After dusting, place all the items back.

Using ammonia, Windex®, or vinegar, dust the mirrors and glass panes.

Washing Windows

Do not wash windows when the sun is shining directly on them because they will dry too quickly and leave streaks.

Before washing the windows, dust the screens, glass, and woodwork. It is best for one person to work outside and one person to work inside.

You can use any of the following as a window cleaner:

- ¼ Cup Household Ammonia to 4 Quarts of Warm Water
- ½ Cup Denatured Alcohol to 4 Quarts of Warm Water
- ½ Cup Vinegar to 4 Quarts of Water

Don't use ammonia and vinegar together.

Dip your lint-free cloth in the bucket of cleaning mixture, wring as dry as you can, and wash the window, making sure to get all the corners and window sills. If the person on the outside uses horizontal strokes and the person on the inside uses vertical strokes, it will make it easier to catch streaks and know where they are. Be sure to get the corners.

Floors

Floors should be swept and vacuumed every day. Dirt builds up so quickly, especially in a house filled with children.

Wipe up spills when they happen and mop at least once a week.

For **wood floors**, dust mop them often to keep dust, debris, and pet hair. For periodic deep cleaning, you can use a wood cleaning product like Murphey's Oil Soap. Use a rag or sponge mop, soaked in the oil soap and rung out so the rag is damp, not wet. Mop the entire floor, rinse off mop with warm water, and squeeze the water out. Use the water-dampened mop to rinse away the soap. Wipe u pany excess water.

Tile floors should be swept or vacuumed a few times a week. For deeper cleaning, use warm water with a little bit of Dawn® dish detergent in it. Don't use a sponge mop—it will just move all the dirt to the grout. Use a rag or a chamois mop to mop the floor. Change the water often so you don't leave a dirty film of water on the tile floor.

Do not sweep **laminate floors**; instead, use a dry mop or a vacuum to get rid of dust, debris, and pet hair. Brooms can scratch a laminate floor. Clean with a vinegar/hot water or ammonia/hot water solution using a damp mop. Make sure the mop is not wet.

Wash Dishes

Before you begin, rinse food off and wipe off any grease with a paper towel. Fill your sink with warm sudsy water and start with all glassware. Wash and rinse. Next the silverware is washed and rinsed. The plates, bowls, and cups are washed and rinsed. Finally, wash the pans and kitchen utensils. Change out water as needed.

Clean up Kitchen

The kitchen should be cleaned each evening so you can wake up to a sparkly kitchen. Here is what needs to be done each night.

- Wash Dishes and put them away
- Wipe down counter-tops, stove, oven, and refrigerator
- Clean sink
- Hang towels and wash cloth to dry
- Sweep floor

Here are the things that need to be cleaned in the kitchen every week:

- Wipe down the front of all appliances.
- Wipe down the front of all cabinets.
- Wipe down the range hood.
- Scrub out the sink and wipe down the faucet.

- Mop the floor.
- Clean the inside and outside of the garbage can.
- Clean or wash sponges and other cleaning towels. I often put spongues in the dishwasher to clean and sterilize them.
- Clean the windows and wipe down the windowsills.
- Tidy pantry.

Here are things that need to be cleaned once a month in the kitchen:

- Wipe down interior cabinet shelves.
- Clean behind the stove and the refrigerator.
- Wipe down baseboards.
- Wipe down the walls.
- Clean the seals on the dishwasher, refrigerator, and garbage disposal with a toothbrush.
- Dust the light fixtures and vent covers. Clean the switch plate.
- Organize pots and pans, or other frequently-used items in cabinets.
- Clean the insides of utensil holders.
- Clean the top of the refrigerator.

Clean up Family Room

The Family Room is where most of the living in done in a household.

- Dust
- Vacuum the carpet or dry mop the floor
- Wipe TV and around door

Clean up Bathroom

When cleaning bathrooms, start with the cleanest part of the bathroom and go step-by-step to the dirtiest.

- Clean Sinks and Counters
- Clean Tub & Shower
- Clean Toilet
- Sweep & Mop Floor

My House Cleaning Plan

You will make a cleaning plan for your family to clean your house. You will have to decide what needs to be done and how it be done, as well as who will do what. You will also need to schedule the cleaning tasks.

Jobs to be Do & How to Do Them

List the jobs that need to be done. I will give you an example.

_____Wash the windows_____   _____We will use a vinegar/water mixture to clean.
One person will clean outside and one inside using a lint-free rag._____

_____
_____

_____   _____
_____
_____

_____   _____
_____
_____

_____   _____
_____
_____

_____   _____
_____
_____

_____   _____
_____
_____

Who Will Do Them

List the chores and who will do them.

_____   _____

_____   _____

_____   _____

_____   _____

_____   _____

_____   _____

_____   _____

_____   _____

When and in What Order

Make a schedule: list the cleaning chores in order of how they will be done. Some jobs can be done at the same time if different family members are doing them.

Time: _____

Jobs: _____
_____
_____

Time: _____

Jobs: _____
_____
_____

Time: _____

Jobs: _____
_____
_____

Time: _____

Jobs: _____
_____
_____

Photo of Me Doing the Family's Laundry

You will do the family laundry this week, sorting, stain treatment, wash, dry, fold, and put away.

Photo of Me Leading Family Cleaning Day

Cleaning Schedules

Many homemakers set up a cleaning schedule.

They might clean a different room every day.

Our schedule was for the whole family to work together on Saturday mornings to clean the entire house.

Talk to your mother and grandmother. Do they have a cleaning schedule? What is their cleaning schedule?

My Mom's Cleaning Schedule: _____
_____
_____
_____
_____
_____
_____

My Grandmother's Cleaning Schedule: _____
_____
_____
_____
_____
_____

Tidy & Clean Family Home

This week you are going to get to tidy and clean your home. Take a photograph of yourself cleaning the house. Write down the things you did to clean the house.

_____	_____	_____
_____	_____	_____
_____	_____	_____
_____	_____	_____
_____	_____	_____
_____	_____	_____
_____	_____	_____

Make a House Cleaning Plan & Administrate a Family Cleaning Day

Now, you have a different assignment. After you cleaned your house by yourself, you have an idea of what needs to be done.

Make a cleaning plan that includes every member of the family.

Family Member: _____

Jobs: _____   _____   _____

_____   _____   _____

_____   _____   _____

Family Member: _____

Jobs: _____   _____   _____

_____   _____   _____

_____   _____   _____

Family Member: _____

Jobs: _____   _____   _____

_____   _____   _____

_____   _____   _____

Family Member: _____

Jobs: _____   _____   _____

_____   _____   _____

_____   _____   _____

Family Member: _____

Jobs: _____   _____   _____

_____   _____   _____

_____   _____   _____

Family Member: _____

Jobs: _____   _____   _____

_____   _____   _____

_____   _____   _____

Family Member: _____

Jobs: _____   _____   _____

_____   _____   _____

_____   _____   _____

Family Member: _____

Jobs: _____   _____   _____

_____   _____   _____

_____   _____   _____

You will need to make a schedule of who does what when.

Here is the cleaning plan for our family:

_____
_____
_____
_____
_____
_____
_____
_____
_____
_____
_____
_____
_____
_____
_____
_____
_____
_____

Here is a photo of the family cleaning:

Week Two Meet with Mom

Recite Proverbs 31.

Discuss Tidying, Organizing, & Cleaning

- Which of the 3 do you like best? Why?
- How did the Family Cleaning Day go? What was good? Bad? What would you do differently?

Share homemaker schedules. Are they really practical?

Make Homemade Lip Gloss. These make great Christmas and birthday presents.

Prayer Focus:

- Prayer Life

Homemade Flavored Lip Gloss

Vaseline® Petroleum Jelly

Crystal Light Granules (choose by flavor and color)

Small Container

Plastic Knife

In a small container, mix the Vaseline® and add some Crystal light granules with a plastic knife. Keep adding granules until you get the color you like.

These make great Christmas presents.

Week Two Home

Memorize Proverbs 31:10-31

Write Proverbs 31:10-31 in the version of your choice. I recommend NASB or NKJ or ESV. Then say the passage aloud.

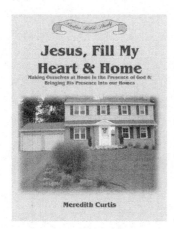

Jesus, Fill My Heart & Home Lesson 8

"Home, a Reflection of Heaven, A Prepared Place"

Read and Answer Questions

My Room, a Haven of Peace, a Reflection of Me

One day you will have your own home, but right now you have a bedroom. Even if you share it with a sibling, that is your special place. You can make your bedroom a home, a place that welcomes you when you walk through the door.

You may have already created your own haven of peace, but if you haven't, look around and plan ways to make your bedroom a cheerful, restful place to be.

Preparing your bedroom will include organizing, tidying, cleaning, and decorating.

Organize Your Room for Rest/Relaxation

The main purpose of a bedroom is a peaceful place for you to relax and sleep. Is your bed comfortable? Is your room peaceful? Do you feel relaxed when you walk through the door of your bedroom? If not, why?

If your room is messy, organize and tidy it.

Is there too much clutter? De-clutter and rearrange things so that you like how it looks.

Is it too sterile? Go ahead and decorate it to reflect the real you.

Does your room make you feel relaxed enough to rest and sleep? If not, why not? Blues, pastels, blue-greens, and bluish-purples create a peaceful atmosphere.

This is your space—it should reflect you and the things you love.

You may not be able to afford a new bedspread and curtains, but you might be able to make some throw pillows or a wall hanging to brighten it up. Maybe Mom and Dad would let you paint your walls or put up a border.

Organize Your Room for Efficiency

What do you use your room for? Is it just to sleep at night and take naps? Do you use your room for reading, listening to music, or doing homework?

Make a list of all the things you do in your room:

_____   _____

_____   _____

_____   _____

_____   _____

_____   _____

Now, think about how well your room is set up to do those things?

If you like to read while you lay down on the bed, is there enough light for you to see? Or do you have a comfortable chair that you can relax in to read? Is there a light nearby?

Do you like to do homework in your room? You might want to set up a little work station for homework with a desk, study lamp, and shelves for books. If you have a desk in your room, you need to make sure the lighting is bright enough so that you do not strain your eyes.

If you like to paint, draw, do crafts, or play music, you might want to set up a little area to do those things in your room, provided your parents approve.

Review how to make the bed and change the bed. Make the bed neatly every day. This will keep your room looking tidy.

Straighten Your Bedroom

Your clothes will last longer if you do not throw them on the floor, bed, or dresser. Instead, fold clean clothes neatly and put them away in your dresser and closet. Put all dirty clothes in a laundry hamper. Make sure that you let damp clothes dry before you put them away. Damp clothes can cause mildew. If clothing becomes mildewed, it must be thrown away.

Organize Your Closet

Closets can get out of control and before you know it, your closet is a wild jungle. The thought of cleaning it out is overwhelming.

A tidy, organized closet is worth investing time and energy to achieve.

First, get rid of clothing that doesn't fit, is ripped, or you haven't worn in several years.

Second, hang clothing purposefully by grouping like with like. Shirts together, skirts together, dresses together.

Third, fold sweaters and jeans and place them on closet shelves.

Fourth, organize shoes neatly and with easy access. You might want to use small shelves or a shoe rack.

Fifth, hang or shelve bags and purses.

Organize Your Dresser Tops & Drawers

Drawers can get out of control, too. Let's organize your drawers.

First divide clothes into different drawers. I use one drawer for shirts, another for shorts, one for swimsuits, and another drawer for scarves and jewelry.

How about you? How do you organize your drawers? _____
_____
_____
_____

Fold your clothes and makes sure they are stacked neat and tidy.

Do You Like Your Room?

Do you like your room? _____
_____

What do you like about your room? _____
_____
_____

What do you want to change about your room? _____
_____
_____

Ways Your Room Can Reflect Your Personality

Does your room reflect your personality? _____
_____
_____
_____

How does your room reflect your personality? _____
_____
_____
_____
_____
_____

What changes would you like to make to reflect your personality? _____
_____
_____
_____
_____
_____

Organize, Tidy, & Clean Your Room

This week you will organize your room. You will also tidy it and clean the bedroom.

Take before and after pictures.

Before Organizing, Tidying, & Cleaning My Room

Re-Arrange & Decorate Your Room

Do you want to make any changes to your room? Move the furniture around? Purchase or make things to decorate your room?

A Photo After Organizing, Tidying, & Cleaning My Room

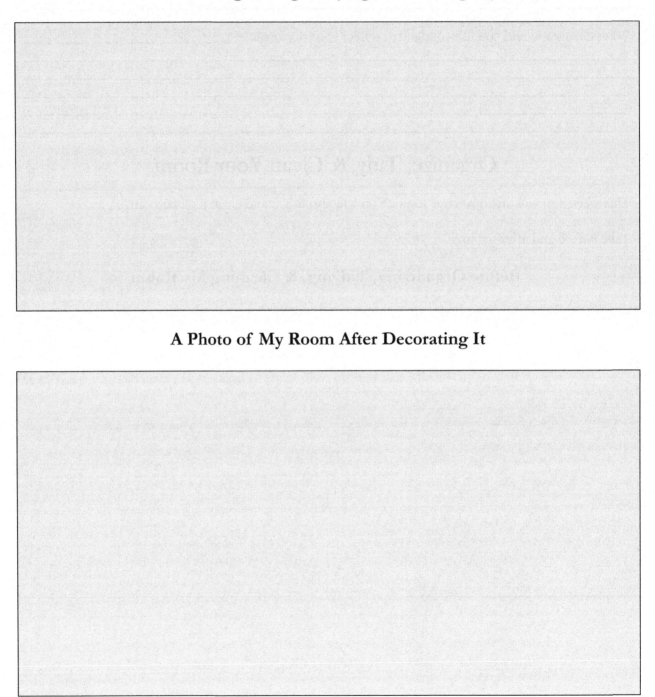

A Photo of My Room After Decorating It

Week Three Meet with Mom

Recite Proverbs 31.

Discuss *Jesus, Fill My Heart & Home*

- What is Heaven like?
- What did God do to make it beautiful and perfect for us to live in forever?
- Do you want to reflect Heaven in your own home?

Discuss Your Room

- What things did you learn about yourself in organizing, cleaning, and considering redecorating your room?
- Do you have any new plans for your room?

Serge Holiday Napkins

Prayer Focus:

- Thanksgiving—reaching out in love to people.

Make a Set of Four Cloth Napkins with a Serger

Supplies:

1¼ Yards Linen, Cotton, or Cotton Blend Fabric

Matching Thread

Tools:

Overlock Sewing Machine

Iron

Scissors

Tape Measure or Ruler

Wash, dry, and iron flat the fabric.

Measure carefully and cut fabric into four 18" x 18" squares.

Set your Overlock Sewing Machine (serger) to make a Rolled Hem while cutting of the excess fabric. Use your sewing machine's instructions to set everything up correctly. With right side of fabric up, hem all four sides in one circuit. Clip all threads. I always add a dap of Fray Check wherever I cut threads. You can buy Fray Check at a fabric or sewing store. It looks like liquid glue.

Repeat for the remaining three napkins.

Make a Set of Four Cloth Napkins with a Sewing Machine

Supplies:

1¼ Yards Linen, Cotton, or Cotton Blend Fabric

Matching Thread

2 Dozen Straight Pins

Tools:

Sewing Machine

Iron

Scissors

Washable pen/marker

Tape Measure or Ruler

Wash, dry, and iron flat the fabric. Measure carefully and cut fabric into four 18" x 18" squares.

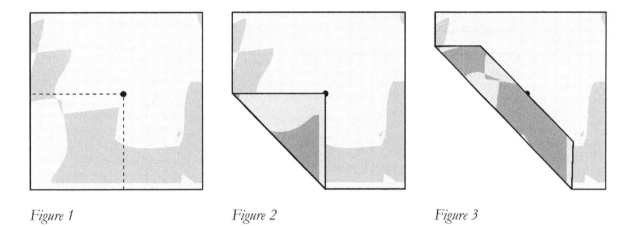

Figure 1   *Figure 2*   *Figure 3*

At the corner, measure one inch from each side and mark the point of intersection on the wrong side of the fabric. With wrong side of the fabric up, fold corner up to this point, press the fold with a hot iron, then fold again so that the pressed fold is now touching the marks on the wrong side of the fabric. Repeat for all the other corners.

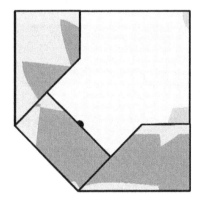
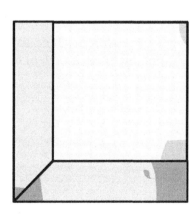

Figure 4   *Figure 5*

Using the ruler to measure, fold up each edge exactly ½" and secure with several pins. Be careful to tuck in the folded corner before pressing creases flat. After all four edges are pressed, measure and fold each edge up another ½"; pin and press. These folded edges should line up at each corner like Figure 5.

Starting at one corner, place napkin on sewing machine, right side up. Stick with a finishing stitch ¼" from the edge pivoting at each corner. Turn the fourth corner and stitch a few more stitches right over the first three to lock them in.

Repeat for three more napkins.

Whether you use a serger or sewing machine to make your napkins, I suggest Scotch Guard® to keep them stain-free. You simply spray it on and let it dry.

Week Three Home

Memorize Proverbs 31:10-31

Write Proverbs 31:10-31 in the version of your choice. I recommend NASB or NKJ or ESV. Then say the passage aloud.

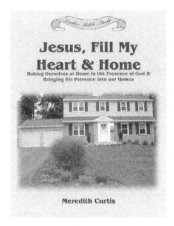

Jesus, Fill My Heart & Home Lesson 9

"How God Decorates & How We Decorate"

Read and Answer Questions

Interior Decorating

Homemaking is preparing and maintaining a home for those you love. It is a ministry unto the Lord and a service for your family. What a great privilege it is to create a home!

Read The Hidden Art of Homemaking, Chapter #5

How does God display His ability as a Decorator? _____
_____
_____
_____
_____

What is His artwork as a Decorator? _____
_____
_____
_____
_____
_____

The way we decorate our home reveals our personalities, interests, and affections. Interior decorating is a fun way to express the creative artist within.

"The next day John was there again with two of his disciples. When he saw Jesus passing by, he said, 'Look, the Lamb of God!'

"When the two disciples heard him say this, they followed Jesus. Turning around, Jesus saw them following and asked, 'What do you want?'

"They said, 'Rabbi' (which means teacher), 'Where are you staying?'

'Come," He replied, *"And you will see.'*

"So they went with Him and saw where He was staying, and spent that day with him. It was about the tenth hour.

"Andrew, Simon Peter's brother, was one of the two who heard what John had said and who had followed Jesus. The first thing Andrew did was to find his brother Simon and tell him, 'We have found the Messiah' (that is, the Christ). And he brought him to Jesus" (John 1:35-41 NIV ©1979).

What do John's disciples ask of Jesus? _____
_____

What is the result of them going home with Him for the day? _____
_____
_____
_____
_____

There is something about where you live that reveals who you are. That's why leaders are to be hospitable people.

"The wise woman builds her house, but with her own hands a foolish woman tears hers down" (Proverbs 14:1 NIV).

How do we build our homes? _____
_____
_____
_____

How do we tear them down? _____
_____
_____
_____

Rooms to Go is such a popular store because all the furniture is already matched up together. But, don't worry. You can learn to put together a room of furniture and accessories.

Please remember the principle of faithful in little, faithful in much. If we are faithful in managing our homes for God's glory, God will increase what we are responsible for.

If we decorate our little apartments for the glory of Christ, we may find ourselves a few years later decorating our own home for His glory.

Remember the principles:

1. We are His Artwork
2. We are beloved.
3. We imitate God when we are creative and we enjoy art and beauty!
4. Christians, above all others should live creatively, artistically, and aesthetically.

Look at God's homemaking in the home He created for us, Heaven.

Think of the principles we learned earlier this year: color, use of light, line, form, unity, dominance (focal point), and others. How does God use these elements of art and principles of design to decorate heaven? Read this passage first to discover the answer.

"Then I saw a new heaven and a new earth, for the first heaven and the first earth had passed away, and there was no longer any sea. I saw the Holy City, the New Jerusalem, coming down out of heaven from God, prepared as a bride beautifully dressed for her husband. And I heard a loud voice from the throne saying, 'Now the dwelling of God is with men, and he will live with them. They will be his people, and God himself will be with them and be their God. He will wipe every tear from their eyes. There will be no more death or mourning or crying or pain, for the old order of things has passed away.'

"He who was seated on the throne said, 'I am making everything new!' Then He said, 'Write this down, for these words are trustworthy and true.' He said to me: 'It is done. I am the Alpha and the Omega, the Beginning and the End. To him who is thirsty I will give to drink without cost from the spring of the water of life. He who overcomes will inherit all this, and I will be his God and He will be my son. But the cowardly, the unbelieving, the vile, the murderers, the sexually immoral, those who practice magic arts, the idolaters, and all liars—their place will be in the fiery lake of burning sulfur. This is the second death.'

"One of the seven angels who had the seven bowls full of the seven last plagues came and said to me, 'Come, I will show you the bride of the Lamb.' And he carried me away in the Spirit to a mountain great and high, and showed me the Holy City, Jerusalem, coming down out of heaven from God. It shone with the glory of God, and its brilliance was like that of a very precious jewel, like a jasper, clear as crystal. It had a great, high wall with twelve gates, and with twelve angels at the gates. On the gates were written the names of the twelve tribes of Israel. There were three gates on the east, three on the north, three on the south and three on the west. The wall of the city had twelve foundations and on them were the names of the twelve apostles of the Lamb.

"The angel who talked with me had a measuring rod of gold to measure the city, its gates and its walls. The city was laid out like a square, as long as it was wide. He measured the city with the rod and found it to be 12,000 stadia in length, and as wide and high as it is long. He measured its wall and it was 144 cubits thick by man's measurement which the angel was using. The wall was made of jasper, and the city of pure god, as pure as glass. The foundations of the city walls were decorated with every kind of precious stone. The first foundations was jasper, the second sapphire, the third chalcedony, the fourth emerald, the fifth sardonyx, the sixth carnelian, the seventh chrysolite, the eighth beryl, the ninth topaz, the tenth chrysoprase, the eleventh jacinth, and the twelfth amethyst. The twelve gates were twelve pearls. The great street of the city was of pure gold, like transparent glass.

"I did not see a temple in the city because the Lord God Almighty and the Lamb are its temple. The city does not need the sun or the moon to shine on it for the glory of God gives it light, and the Lamb is its lamp. The nations will walk by its light, and the kings of the earth will bring their splendor into it. On no day will its gates ever be shut, for there will be no night there. The glory and honor of the nations will be brought into it. Nothing impure will every enter it, nor will anyone who does what is shameful or deceitful, but only those whose names are written in the Lamb's book of life.

"Then the angel showed me the river of the water of life, as clear as crystal, flowing from the throne of God and of the lamb down the middle of the great street of the city. On each side of the river stood the tree of life, bearing twelve crops of fruit, yielding its fruit every month. And the leaves of the tree are for the healing of the nations. No longer will there be any curse. The throne of God and of the Lamb will be in the city, and his servants will serve him. They will see his *face, and his name will be on their foreheads. There will be no more night. They will not need the light of a lamp or the light of the sun, for the Lord God will give them light. And they will reign forever and ever"* (Revelation 21:1-22:5 NIV©1979).

How does God use these elements of art (line, color, texture, form, media) **and principles of design** (balance, dominance, proportion, unity, rhythm) **to decorate heaven?**

_____
_____
_____
_____
_____

We imitate God by making Jesus the focal point. In Heaven, JESUS is the Focal Point.

Remember principle: Art reflects the character and personality of the artist. What we have in common is that we are all servants of Christ. But, each homemaker is unique with her own tastes, calling, vocation, gifts, talents, ministries, and hobbies.

Here are the steps to decorate your home.

1. Prayer

2. Thank the Lord for your house. Dedicate it to Him. Ask Him for His creativity and loveliness to flow through you. Ask for wisdom.

3. Decorating Style/Discover what you really like and what will reflect your heart.

    A. Visit all the nice stores: furniture, antique stores, gift shops, art galleries.

    B. Pile of magazines. Tear out pages that you like.

    C. Now look for common themes: colors schemes, ambiance, lighting

    Do you like rustic? Country? Cluttered and cozy? Sleek and modern? Victorian?

4. Treasure hunt through your house.

5. Organize clutter—make your storage cute!

6. Clean house

7. Practical considerations. Does everything do what it is supposed to do?

8. Pray: "Lord Jesus, are you pleased with this room?"

Color

There are warm and cool colors. The hue is the color name. The value is how light or dark a color is. You tint with white and shade with black.

Intensity is the strength or purity of a color. You can mute (reduce intensity) by mixing with its compliment.

When you decorate with colors, you can use a complementary color scheme (opposites on color wheel) such as yellow and purple. Or you can use an adjacent (analogous) color scheme with colors that are next to each other on the color wheel such as purple, blue, and green.

If you use a monochromatic color scheme (just one color), you will employ different values, tones and textures of one color.

A split-complementary scheme employs a color with the 2 color adjacent to its opposite complement (blue with red-orange and yellow-orange) on a color wheel.

Color schemes can be four or more colors but are usually 2-3. I usually use one main color and one to two accent colors.

Keep These Principles in Mind

Proportion/Balance: Contrast and variety balanced with symmetry and unity. Shapes should be harmonious to space. A small couch in a small room and a large couch in a large room.

Focal Point, or Focus of Room: Bed, fireplace, dining room table are natural focal points. If no natural one, create one on the impact wall.

Unity/Rhythm: Consistent mood. Whole picture should "work" Emphasize the positive and eliminate or camouflage the negative.

Function: Comfort. Purpose of room.

Christian Symbols: Cross, fish, IXOYE (Ikthus is Greek word for fish and means Jesus, Christ, God's Son, Savior), Bread of Life, True Vine, Dove, Rose,

"Hear, O Israel: The Lord our God, the LORD is one. Love the LORD your God with all your heart, and with all your soul, and with all your strength. These commandments that I give you today are to be upon your hearts. Impress them on your children. Talk about them when you sit at home and when you walk along the road, when you lie down and when you get up. Tie them as symbols on your hands and bind them on your foreheads. Write them on the doorframes of your houses and on your gates" (Deuteronomy 6:4-9 NIV ©1979).

Get rid of anti-Christian symbols. The Israelites were commanded to write Scriptures on the doorframes of their homes. That is a pattern for us. We certainly don't want to do the opposite and dishonor Christ with our decorating.

Architectural Styles

Log Cabin

Log cabins, originally from Sweden, have dotted America since the 1600s. They are usually found in a rural setting.

Cape Cod

Cape Cods, another style dating back to the 1600s, was inspired by British thatched cottages, but with steeper roofs and larger chimneys needed for the cold New England winters. Cape cods have windows on each side, dormer windows on the second story, and a shingled roof.

Art Deco

Art Deco is an art and architectural style from the early twentieth century. These homes have flat roofs, smooth stucco walls with rounded corners, and bold decorations on the outside.

Bungalow or Craftsman

Made from natural materials like wood, stone, and brick, these homes are built with wide front porches, low roofs, and an open floor plan. The inside often includes exposed beams and large fireplaces.

Colonial

Colonial homes date back to early colonial times (1600s) and are renowned for their symmetry: evenly spaced shuttered windows, dormers, and evenly spaced columns. Colonial homes are very formal in appearance.

Greek Revival

Inspired by the Ancient Greeks, Greek Revival homes were popular in the 1830s and 1840s. Symmetrical with a formal style, Greek Revivals have large columns, spacious porches, and painted plaster exteriors. Greek Revivals were often found on large plantations.

Mediterranean

Popular in the early 1900s and influenced by Mediterranean countries, Mediterranean homes have red tile roofs, arches, and plaster surfaces. Heavy wooden doors, porticos, balconies, ornamental details, and multicolored tiles make these homes quite impressive!

Ranch

Ranch homes were first built in the 1930s, modeled after rural Western ranch homes. The one-story floor plans are open with easy access to the outdoors.

Victorian

Victorian homes were popular between 1830 and 1910 with their ornate trim, large porches, bright colors, and multi-faceted rooflines.

Cottage

Cotters, European peasants famers in the Middle Ages lived in little homes. Named after the cotters, these small homes are built of stone or wood siding, often have a covered entryway, and are painted in bright colors.

Farmhouse

Farmhouses were built on farms, modeled after the popular styles of the time such as Colonial or Victorian. Farmhouses were built to be functional and have large porches.

Your Favorite Style

After learning about these different house styles, which is your favorite?

_____

Decorating Styles

There are many different decorating styles. Do you have a favorite?

Let's explore some different decorating styles.

Coastal Style

The Coastal Style is comfortable, inviting, and a tribute to the surf, sand, and sun. Use boats, wicker, driftwood, shells, rope, rowing oars, sailboats, lighthouses, and photos with a beach and nautical themes to decorate in the Coastal Style. Striped fabric, especially blue and white fits in perfectly.

French Country Style

Rustic and refined collide in the French Country style with lots of wood and ruffles.

Shabby Chic

Vintage furniture and elements combine to create an antique store feel in Shabby Chic. The most popular colors are white, ecru, and pastels.

Cottage Style

Cozy and charming are the best words to describe Cottage Style. Simple treasure pieces, even if they are tattered and mismatched, create a warm sense of home.

Contemporary

The Contemporary Style is neutral, clean, smooth, subtle, and clutter-free. Straight lines predominate in this sterile décor.

Eclectic

Breaking rules, mixing styles, and expressing the owners taste freely defines the Eclectic styles of decorating.

Other Styles include Early American, Colonial, Gothic, Scandinavian, Modern, Tuscan, Minimalist, Mid-Century Modern, English Country, Medieval, Spanish, Southwestern, Art Deco, Art Nouveau, Arabian, Shaker, Chinese, Moroccan, and Japanese. You can explore these on your own.

Which style do you like best? _____

Color Combinations

You have probably seen a color wheel before.

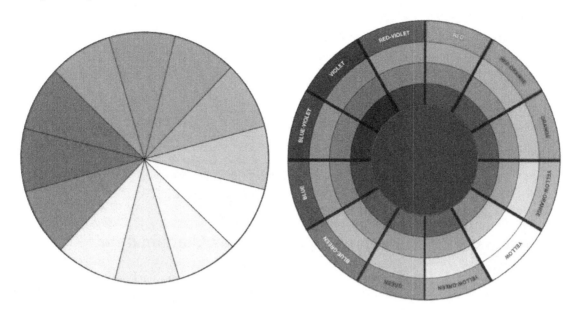

Color Scheme #1: Complementary Colors

Choose colors that are across from one another like blue and orange, purple and yellow, and red and green.

Name some other color combinations:

_____   +   _____

_____   +   _____

_____   +   _____

What is your favorite Complementary Color Combination?

_____   +   _____

Color Scheme #2: Three Color Triangle Combination

Choose colors that form a triangle with one another like purple, orange, and green.

Name some three-color triangle combinations:

_____   +   _____   +   _____

_____   +   _____   +   _____

What is your favorite Three Color Triangle Combination?

_____   +   _____

Color Scheme #3: Three Color Adjacent Color Combination

Choose colors that are next to each other like purple, blue-purple, and green.

Name some three-color triangle combinations:

_____   +   _____   +   _____

_____   +   _____   +   _____

What is your favorite three -color adjacent color combination?

_____   +   _____

Color Scheme #4: Split Complementary Color Combination

In this combination, you take one primary color and the two colors on each side of the color straight across the wheel from the primary color. One combination is blue with red-orange and yellow-orange.

Name the other two split complementary color combinations:

_____   +   _____   +   _____

_____   +   _____   +   _____

What is your favorite split complementary color combination?

_____   +   _____

Other Color Combinations

There are several other color combinations that work nicely with one another. Here is a list of my favorites:

- White combines with everything especially blue, black, and red
- Beige goes nicely with blue, brown, green, black, red, and white
- Pink combines nicely with white, mint green, turquoise, light blue, navy, brown, black, and gray
- Raspberry looks great with white, black, and damask rose
- Yellow combines nicely with white, blue, lilac, violet, gray, and black

What are your favorite color combinations?

_____   +   _____

_____   +   _____

_____   +   _____

_____ + _____ + _____

_____ + _____ + _____

Cut out some pictures of color schemes you like and paste in the box below.

Holiday Recipes & Family Favorites

Most families have favorite holiday dishes that they look forward to eating at Thanksgiving, Christmas, Easter, and other holidays.

How about your family? What are some favorite foods and desserts that you and your family enjoy at the holidays?

Thanksgiving Favorites

_____

_____

_____

_____

_____

Christmas Favorites

_____

_____

_____

_____

_____

Easter Favorites

_____

_____

_____

_____

_____

Other Holiday and Birthday Favorites

_____

_____

_____

_____

_____

_____

_____

_____

_____

_____

_____

Now get the recipes from your mom or other relative. Write them on index cards. Add them to your Special Recipe Box. You might want to make some of those special dishes at Thanksgiving or Christmas.

Prepare the Turkey for Thanksgiving

This Thanksgiving, you will cook the turkey for Thanksgiving. Let your mom or dad coach you through it, but do it yourself. If you want directions, they are on the next page.

After you make the turkey, share about your experience here:

_____
_____
_____
_____
_____
_____
_____
_____
_____

How to Cook a Turkey

Frozen or Fresh Turkey (2 pounds per person will give you plenty to eat and leftovers)

1 Large Onion

5 Cloves Garlic

Salt, Pepper, & Garlic Powder to Taste

If frozen, thaw turkey in the refrigerator. Allow 1 day for every 4-5 pounds. That means it would take 3 days to thaw a 15-pound turkey.

Remove the neck and giblets. Rinse the cavity well. Place in large roasting pan. If stuffing the turkey, lightly spoon stuffing into the bird's cavity. Pack stuffing loosely. If not, place a large onion and 5 cloves of garlic inside the cavity to add flavor to the bird. Sprinkle skin with salt, pepper, and garlic powder. Cover bird with foil

Preheat oven to 325° and roast turkey 15-20 minutes per pound. A 15 pound bird would take 4-5 hours to cook. To see if turkey is done, place a meat thermometer into the thickest part of the bird. Temperature should be above 165°. Many turkeys have a temperature gauge that pops up when the turkey is done.

Remove turkey from oven and let sit for 1 hour, covered loosely with foil.

To carve the turkey, follow these steps.

1. Remove the legs. Slice through the skin between the body and leg. Pull leg outward so you can cut through the hip joint.
2. Remove the breast from the turkey.
3. Place breast on cutting board and slice breast.
4. Separate the leg from the thigh. Serve drumsticks whole.
5. Slice the thighs.
6. Remove wings from backbone and serve wings whole.

Uses for leftover turkey

- Late night turkey sandwiches
- Turkey tacos
- Turkey casseroles
- Turkey Soup
- Turkey Salad

Beautiful Home on a Budget Book Review

By Emilie Barnes & Yoli Brogger

What is your style?

_____
_____
_____
_____
_____

What are the rules of decorating?

_____
_____
_____
_____
_____

Which rules would you like to break?

_____
_____
_____
_____
_____
_____

What is the focus, or anchor, or a room?

_____
_____
_____
_____

How can you decorate walls in a house?

_____
_____
_____
_____
_____

Share 10 decorating tips/ideas that you loved!

_____
_____

_____

_____
_____

_____
_____

_____
_____

_____
_____

_____
_____

_____
_____

_____
_____

What are your favorite colors for decorating?

_____
_____
_____
_____

What can you do with fabric in a house?

_____
_____
_____
_____
_____

December: Interior Decorating

Memorize Proverbs 31

Jesus, Fill My Heart & Home Bible Study

Hidden Art of Homemaking

Dream House Project

Cookies, Cake Decorating

Gardening

Optional: *Building Her House Well* Book Review

(Meet with Mom weekly)

Week One Meet with Mom

Recite Proverbs 31.

Discuss Principles of Interior Design

Discuss What You Like & Why (Architecture, Decorating Styles, Colors)

Make a Wreath, Wall Hanging, or Plague that Communicates Welcome

Prayer Focus:

- Families in your church

Welcome Wreath

Today you will make a floral wreath to welcome your family and friends home! You can make one of the wreaths on the following pages or come up with your own ideas.

Making a Floral Wreath

Supplies:

 1 Foam Wreath Form

 Dozens of Small Silk Flowers in Small Bundles in a Variety of Colors

 2 Yards of 3" Wide Fabric Ribbon

 1 Spool of Narrow Satin Ribbon

 1 Small Welcome Sign with Holes for Hanging (or 1" Letters Painted in a Variety of Colors to Spell W-E-L-C-O-M-E)

 2 Dozen Straight Pins

Tools:

 Scissors

 Wire Cutters

Cut the end of the 3" ribbon at a slight angle. Anchor this end of the ribbon to the back of the wreath form with three or four straight pins. Wrap the ribbon somewhat loosely around the wreath again and again overlapping about half the ribbon each time around. Once you have wrapped the wreath completely anchor the ribbon with three or four straight pins and trim off any excess ribbon.

Separate any large bundles of flowers into singles or in bundles of two or three with 2-3" stems. Treating the overlapping ribbon as

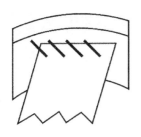

pockets, tuck a single or bundled flower(s) into each pocket, sliding them to the outside of the wreath. Once you have tucked at least one flower in each pocket, repeat the process sliding the flowers to the inside of the wreath. Finally fill in the center of the wreath surfaces with more flowers.

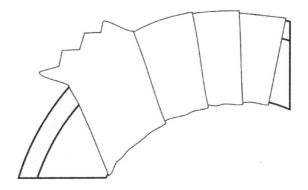

Using the narrow ribbon, tie the sign across the lower center of the wreath opening. Use the straight pins to anchor the ends of the narrow ribbons among the flowers. Alternately you can tie each of the letters together with this ribbon and anchor them the same way.

Using a 12" piece of the narrow ribbon to make a hanger for the wreath. Anchor the ends with straight pins at the back of the wreath form. For an added accent, use the straight pins to anchor the narrow ribbon in several spots around the wreath forming long loops.

Making a Simple Wreath

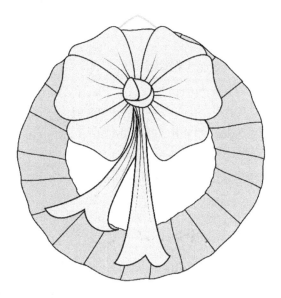

Supplies:

1 Foam Wreath Form

2 Spools Wide Ribbon in Complimentary colors

12" Narrow Ribbon (Matching one of the other Ribbons)

1 Dozen Straight Pins

Tools:

Scissors

Wire Cutters

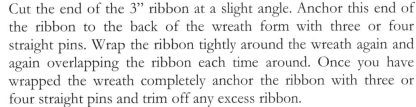

Cut the end of the 3" ribbon at a slight angle. Anchor this end of the ribbon to the back of the wreath form with three or four straight pins. Wrap the ribbon tightly around the wreath again and again overlapping the ribbon each time around. Once you have wrapped the wreath completely anchor the ribbon with three or four straight pins and trim off any excess ribbon.

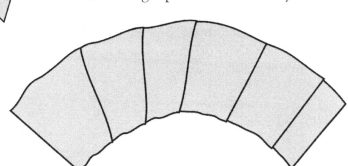

Use the second ribbon to wrap around the wreath once at the top and tie a big bow in the front. Anchor the narrow ribbon on the back of the wreath near the top to form a hanger for the wreath.

Making a FlipFlop Welcome Sign

Supplies:

    4-7 Pairs of Cheap Flip Flops

    4 Decorative Silk or Plastic Large Tropical Flowers or Butterflies

    1 Spool Thin Silk Ribbon to Match One of the Flip Flops

    3-7 Bottles of Puffy Paint

Tools:

    Hot Glue Gun

    Scissors

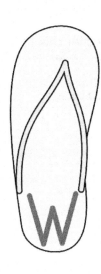

Pick out your favorite 7 flip flops, some lefties, some righties. If you are using all different flip flops line them up in whatever random order you wish. If you are using multiples of matching flip flops, make sure to separate the matches. Take each flip flop and line it up straight up and down. Using the puffy paint, write one of the letters W-E-L-C-O-M or E at the heal of the flip flop so that it too is straight up and down.

After the puffy paint dries glue the first E flip flop to the W flip flop, overlapping, tilting, and offsetting just a little. Next glue the M flip flop to the other E flip flop the same way.

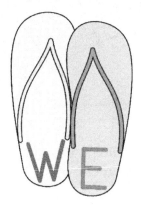

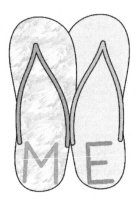

Give the glue a couple minutes to cool and set then glue the L flip flop to the E flip flop, and the O flip flop to the M flip flop following the same pattern.

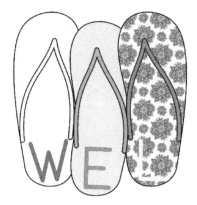

Once the glue has cooled and set for another couple of minutes, pull the two sides together and position them under the C flip flop. Without glue, place the C flip flop on the others to verify placement and identify exactly where you need glue. Work one side of the C flip flop at a time. Apply glue and glue the C flip flop to the L flip flop; let it set a couple minutes then apply glue and attached the C flip flop to the O flip flop.

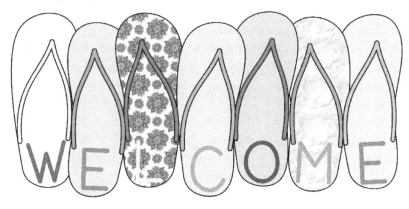

Now that we have all the flip flops glued together, we can attach a string to use for hanging this welcome sign. On the back of your flip flops there should be a plug which holds the thong to the base of the shoe. Give this plug a little tug and tightly tie your thin silk ribbon to the back of the E flip flop. Stretch out the ribbon as much as desired for your hanger then tie the other end of the ribbon to the back of the W flip flop.

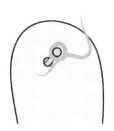

Finally attach the decorative flowers and/or butterflies to the sign as accents.

Week One Home

Memorize Proverbs 31:10-31

Write Proverbs 31:10-31 in the version of your choice. I recommend NASB or NKJ or ESV. Then say the passage aloud.

My Dream House Project

Today, we are going to dream a little. You will need to purchase some home decorating magazines from the grocery store so you can cut out photos to put in each box on the following pages.

Pretend that you are free to design your dream house.

The outside of the house, the gardens, and every room inside.

Think about different homes that you've been in that you really like. Think about the architectural styles and decorating styles.

Our homes, like our bedrooms reflect who we are. Your home should be a place of refuge and peace for your family.

Decorate for the Glory of God

We want to glorify God when we decorate and imitate Him. He makes everything beautiful. Now is your opportunity to start the process of learning to bring beauty into your home for God's glory and to bless your family. In addition, we want to fill our homes with Scripture. Maybe on plagues, or wall hangings, or pillows. Think about ways to honor Christ as you decorate.

In the Future

Today, we are just daydreaming, but it will help you to plan how you want to decorate in the future.

Most families don't have a lot of money to decorate their homes, but there is so much you can do if you are creative.

With yard sale finds, fabric, and a glue gun you can do so many things to make your home beautiful inside and outside.

I have made country lampshades, wall hangings, pillows, welcome wreathes, curtains, stenciled walls, sponged walls, painted old furniture, and refinished furniture. It's fun and easy once you learn how to do it.

Are you ready? Get Set! Decorate your dream house!

My Dream House Front View

My Dream House Garden/Yard

My Dream House Living Room

My Dream House Kitchen

My Dream House Bedrooms

My Dream House Bathrooms

My Dream House Family Room

Week Two Meet with Mom

Recite Proverbs 31.

Share & Discuss Dream House Project

Make an Ornament

Prayer Focus:

- Christmas

Clothespin Reindeers

Supplies:

- ✳ 3 No-roll Clothespins
- ✳ Brown paint
- ✳ 2-5mm googley eyes
- ✳ 1 red 5mm pom-pom
- ✳ 1 white 10mm pom-pom
- ✳ 1' of 1/8" ribbon

Tools:

- ❖ Paper or foam plate
- ❖ Paint brush
- ❖ Scissors
- ❖ Hot glue gun

Instructions:

1. Paint the clothespins brown on every surface.
2. Using the hot glue gun, glue two of the clothespin together at the top. This is the body and legs of your reindeer.
3. Glue the third clothespin, upside down to the first two. This is the head and antlers of your reindeer.

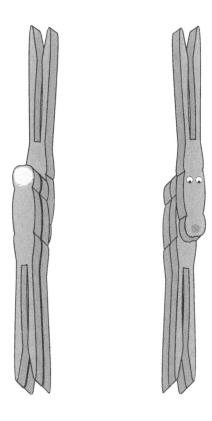

4. Put a dot of hot glue on back side of the reindeer and attach the white pom-pom.

5. Put two tiny dots of hot glue at the middle of the face of the reindeer and attach the googley eyes.

6. Put a dot of hot glue on the lower part of the face and attach the red pom-pom for the nose.

7. Tie the ribbon tightly around the neck of the reindeer with a knot on the back and a slip knot on the end.

Quilted Ball Ornaments

Supplies:

* 3" foam ball
* 40-2 ½" squares of fabric in two different colors (24 of color A, 16 of color B)
* 205 straight pins
* 11" piece of ½" wide ribbon
* 4' piece of ¼" wide ribbon

Tools:

* Scissors

Instructions:

Round 1

1. Finger press a crease down the middle and across the middle of a color A fabric square. This is to find the exact center of the square which is where the pins will be passed through the fabric.

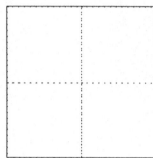

2. Press a pin through the center of the fabric square, so that the pin head is on the wrong or ugly side of the fabric.

3. Push the pin into the foam ball. Fold the fabric in half and secure the bottom corners with two push pins.

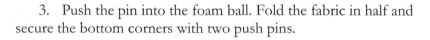
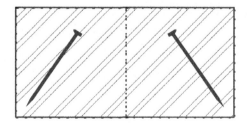

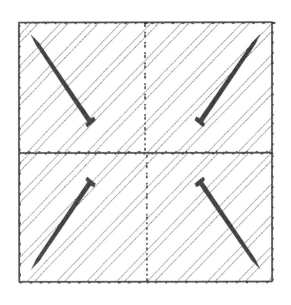

4.   Repeat steps 1- 3 with another color A fabric square, placing the pin right next to the first pin mirroring the first square, forming a full square on one side of the ball.

5.   Fold the top corner of one of the folded squares down toward the center of the bottom of the piece of fabric. Pull the fabric firmly then secure with a straight pin.

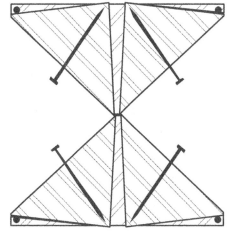

6.   Repeat step 5 with the other corner of this fabric square

7.   Repeat steps 5 & 6 with the other fabric square.

8.   Repeat steps 1-7 with two more fabric squares of color A. They should overlap the first two triangles

9.   Repeat steps 1-8 with four more fabric squares of color A at the exact polar opposite side of the ball. Make sure that the lines created by the fabric squares on one side of the ball line up with the lines created by the fabric squares on the other side of the ball.

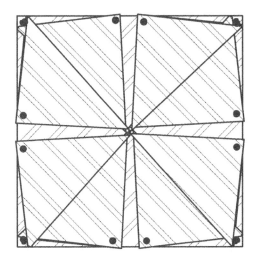

Round 2

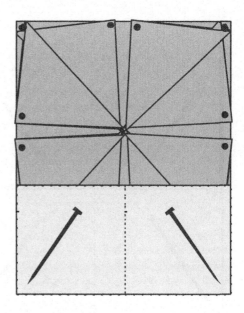

10. Finger press a crease down the middle and across the middle of a color B fabric square.
11. Press a pin through the center of the fabric square, so that the pin head is on the wrong or ugly side of the fabric.
12. Estimate a line that is about ¾" long from the initial pin, along the center line created by the fabric triangle and press the pin into the foam ball. Fold the fabric in half and secure the bottom corners with two push pins.
13. Fold the top corner of the folded square down toward the center of the bottom of the piece of fabric. Pull the fabric firmly then secure with a straight pin.
14. Repeat step 13 with the other top corner.

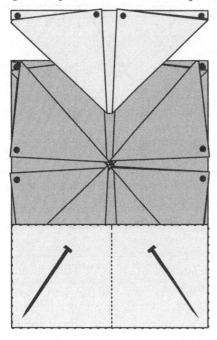

15. Repeat steps 10-14 opposite the first color B square.

16. Repeat steps 10-14 at the remaining two positions of the cross.

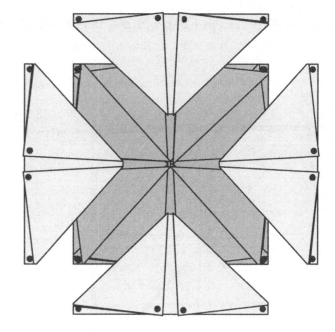

17. Repeat steps 10-16 with four more fabric squares of color B at the exact polar opposite side of the ball. Make sure that the lines created by the fabric squares on one side of the ball line up with the lines created by the fabric squares on the other side of the ball.

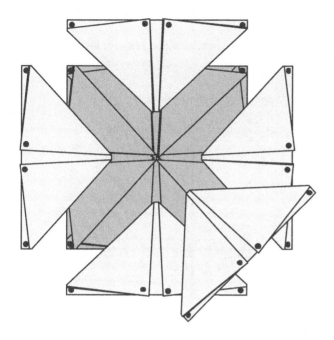

18. Finger press a crease down the middle and across the middle of a color B fabric square.

19. Press a pin through the center of the fabric square, so that the pin head is on the wrong or ugly side of the fabric.

20. Estimate a line that is about ¾" long from the initial pin, along the diagonal line created by the fabric triangles and press the pin into the foam ball. Fold the fabric in half and secure the bottom corners with two push pins. It will overlap the color B triangles just placed along the cross made by the first layer of fabric squares.

21. Fold the top two corners of the folded

square down toward the center of the bottom of the piece of fabric. Pull the fabric firmly then secure with a straight pin.

22. Repeat steps 18-21 for the opposite diagonal.

23. Repeat steps 18-22 for the remaining two diagonals.

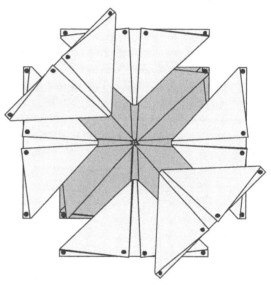

24. Repeat steps 18-23 at the exact polar opposite side of the ball. Make sure that the lines created by the fabric squares on one side of the ball line up with the lines created by the fabric squares on the other side of the ball.

Round 3

25. Finger press a crease down the middle and across the middle of a color A fabric square.

26. Press a pin through the center of the fabric square, so that the pin head is on the wrong or ugly side of the fabric.

27. Estimate a line that is about ½" long

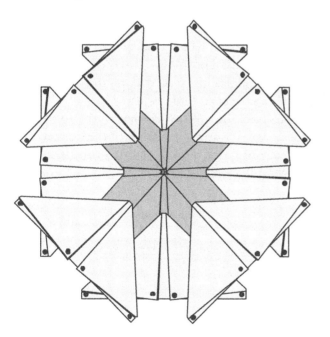

from the tip of a color B triangle, along the center line created by the fabric triangle and press the pin into the foam ball. Fold the fabric in half and secure the bottom corners with two push pins.

28. Fold the top corner of the folded square down toward the center of the bottom of the piece of fabric. Pull the fabric firmly then secure with a straight pin.

29. Repeat step 28 with the other top corner.

30. Repeat steps 25-29 opposite the first color A square of this round.

31. Repeat steps 25-29 at the remaining two positions of the cross.

32. Repeat steps 25-31 with four more fabric squares of color A at the exact polar opposite side of the ball. Make sure that fabric triangles line up with the triangles from the opposite side.

33. Finger press a crease down the middle and across the middle of a color A fabric square.

34. Press a pin through the center of the fabric square, so that the pin head is on the wrong or ugly side of the fabric.

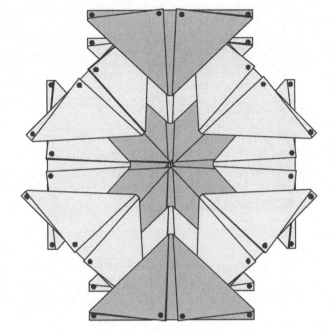

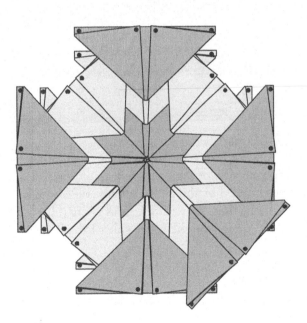

35. Estimate a line that about ½" long from the tip of a color B triangle, along the center line created by the color B fabric triangles on the diagonals and press the pin into the foam ball. Fold the fabric in half and secure the bottom corners with two push pins. It will overlap the color A triangles just placed along the cross made by the first layer of fabric squares.

36. Fold the top two corners of the folded square down toward the center of the bottom of the piece of fabric. Pull the fabric firmly then secure with a straight pin.

37. Repeat steps 33-36 for the opposite diagonal.
38. Repeat steps 33-36 for the remaining two diagonals.
39. Repeat steps 33-38 at the exact polar opposite side of the ball. Make sure that all the triangles line up evenly and barely overlap.
40. Measure ½" from either end of the 10" piece of ribbon and stick two straight pins through the back of each end, so that the pin heads are on the wrong or ugly side of the ribbon.
41. Press two pins into the ornament along the overlapping fabric triangles. Fold the ribbon over the pin heads to hide them and the edge of the ribbon.
42. Wrap the ribbon around the ornament and press the other two pins into the ornament next to the first two, hiding the pins and the other end of the ribbon.

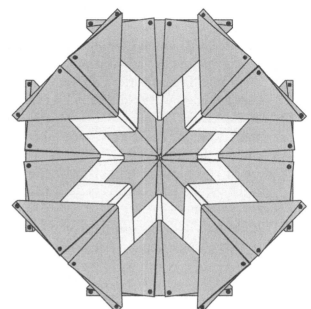

43. Loop the 3/16" ribbon 7 times with 4" extra tails on either end.
44. Press one straight pin through the loops. The pin should pierce the ribbon 8 times.

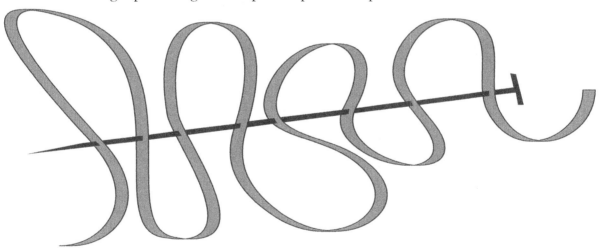

45. Press the straight pin, with the ribbon loops, into the ornament between the four pins securing the wide ribbon. Spread the loops evenly around the ornament top.

Hints

❖ While the diagrams in these instructions are flat, your ornament will be round and therefore, corners will touch in the ornament in places that they do not touch in the diagrams.

❖ A standard "fabric quarter" also known as a "fat quarter" (available at any shop that carries quilting fabrics) will yield 56 2 ½" squares.

❖ An extra strip of color B can be folded into thirds length wise and used as a wide ribbon around the center of the ornament.

❖ Cotton is the easiest to work with, but other fabrics can be used. I have used lamé, colored lace, and even velvet ribbon.

❖ Don't fret if the edges of the fabric squares don't line up perfectly as you go, they will all be covered.

Week Two Home

Memorize Proverbs 31:10-31

Write Proverbs 31:10-31 in the version of your choice. I recommend NASB or NKJ or ESV. Then say the passage aloud.

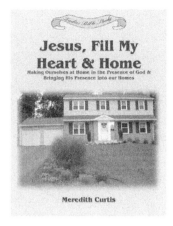

Jesus, Fill My Heart & Home Lesson 10

"Home: A Reflection of Heaven: A Dwelling Place & A Nurturing Center"

Read and Answer Questions

How to Decorate the House for Christmas

This week, it's time to think about celebrating Christmas in your own home with your own family.

What traditions do you love in your own family?

_____

_____

_____

_____

Does your family decorate for Christmas? _____

How do they decorate the outside of the house for Christmas? _____

_____

_____

_____

How does your family decorate the inside of the house for Christmas? _____

_____

_____

_____

_____

_____

What things do you want to continue in your own family? _____

_____

_____

_____

_____

Decorate Outside for Christmas

Here are some tips for decorating the outside of the house for Christmas:

- Hang a wreath on the door
- Decorate doors and windows with greenery
- Hang lights
- Point Poinsettia plants on the porch

Decorate Inside for Christmas

Here are some tips for decorating the inside of the house for Christmas:

- Set up a Nativity Scene
- Add a Christmas tree and decorate with ornaments and garland. Put a tree rug underneath the tree
- Use pine branches as garland on the staircase, fireplace, and table tops
- Use lights and candles in strategic places
- Hang Stockings
- Display Christmas Cards
- Use Christmas tablecloths, napkins, and table runners
- Put candles in the window
- Display a gingerbread house
- Fill a toy wagon with Christmas stuffed animals
- Hang paper snowflakes from the ceiling

Decorate the House for Christmas

This week, you will decorate the house for Christmas, inside and outside. Be create and festive as you put up decorations and get the house ready for Christmas celebrations.

Photos of My Christmas Decorating

Paste photos of your Christmas decorating on this page.

How to Wrap Gifts Creatively

There are many ways to wrap presents creatively. You can use plain brown paper and add ribbon and gold writing. You can use black paper and add white writing. A simple brown paper bag can become festive with a photograph glued to the back. Add something under the ribbon/bow. Use only one color for wrapping and bow, or shades of one color.

Wrap Christmas Presents

Christmas is coming and there are lots of presents to wrap. This week wrap the gifts you are giving to others. Try to do something creative for each gift.

Take a photograph of your gifts and put paste them in the box below.

Cake Decorating 101

This week we will decorate a cake.

Before You Start

Before you start decorating a cake, you might want to practice the following piping patterns:

- Dots
- Stars
- Lines
- Writing
- Pearl Borders
- Shell Borders
- Rosettes
- Ruffles

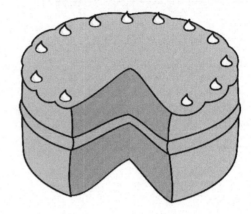

Step #1: Stack the Layers

Start by baking a cake. You can use a mix. Chill the cake layers so they are easier to frost and work with.

Place your first layer on a cake plate on top of a round turntable. If you can't find a turntable, it's okay, but it makes it easier to frost the cake if you can move it around.

Fill a pastry bag fitted with a plain round piping tip with the frosting you will use as the base color of your cake.

Pipe a ring of frosting around the edge of your cake layer. This will create a barrier to keep the frosting from seeping out.

Fill the ring with your choice of filling or frosting and smooth flat with an offset spatula.

Place the next layer on top of the cake and repeat. Continue to stack until you get to the top layer. Step back and look at your cake layers. Is the cake straight? Are any of the layers leaning? Use this time to straighten it out.

Add the top layer upside down. The bottom is flatter and crumb-free.

Step #2: Create the Crumb Coat and Chill

The Crumb coat is the first layer of frosting. It traps all the crumbs.

Smooth out any frosting peeking out of the layers and fill in any gaps.

Use an offset spatula to spread a thin layer of frosting on the sides and top of the cake.

Chill the cake for ten to fifteen minutes.

Step #3: Frost

Remove from the refrigerator and place on the turntable again.

Start with a large dollop of frosting on the top of the cake and smooth it out with an offset spatula. Spin the turntable as you frost the cake so that the layer is even. Frost the sides, making sure the layer of frosting is even.

Once the cake is frosted, hold the spatula perpendicular to the turntable and press gently against the sides of the cake. Spin the turntable to create a smooth layer of frosting on the sides. Do the same on the top.

Chill the cake for ten to fifteen minutes again.

Dip your spatula in hot water and dry it. This will heat the metal. Use the spatula one more time to smooth the frosting.

Step #4: Pipe Borders & Decorations

Fill a piping bag with frosting and the top of your choice. Pipe a border around the edge of the cake at the top and around the bottom. Use various tips to create decorations on top of the cake.

Cookies, Cookies, Cookies

Christmas is the time to bake Christmas cookies.

Candy Cane Cookies

1 ¼ Cup Sugar

1 Cup Butter

1 Egg

½ Cup Milk

1 tsp. Vanilla

1 tsp. Peppermint Extract

3 ½ Cup Flour

1 tsp. Baking Powder

¼ tsp. Salt

½ tsp. Red Food Color (plus more to the color you desire)

Cream together sugar and butter in a large mixing bowl. Add egg, then milk, vanilla, and peppermint extract. Stir in flour, baking powder and salt. Divide dough in half.

Stir food color into one half. Cover and refrigerate at least 4 hours. Preheat oven to 375 ° F. For each candy cane, shape one rounded tsp dough from each half into 4-inch rope by rolling back and forth on clean surface. (Don't use flour or it won't stick to the other half.) Place one red and white rope side by side; press together lightly and twist.

Place on prepared cookie sheet; curve top of cookie down to form handle of cane. Bake 9 to 12 minutes or until set and very light brown. Remove from cookie sheet to wire rack and cool completely.

Roll Out & Cut Out Cookie Recipes

Some bakers chill the dough before they roll it out. Others place the dough between two sheets of waxed paper and roll it out; then they chill the dough before using the cookie cutters.

Gingerbread Man Cookies

6 Cups Flour

1 Tbsp. Baking Soda

1 Tbsp. Ginger

1 tsp. Cloves

1 tsp. Cinnamon

1 tsp. Nutmeg

½ tsp. Salt

1 Cup Shortening

1 Cup Molasses

1 Cup Packed Brown Sugar

½ Cup Water

1 Large Egg

1 tsp. Vanilla

Mix flour, soda, spices, and salt together in a bowl. Beat together shortening, molasses, sugar, water, egg, and vanilla until well blended. Gradually beat in flour mixture. Dough will be soft. Divide dough into fourths. Pat each section of dough in a 1" thick round and refrigerate at least 3 hours (up to a week). Roll out on a lightly floured surface to 1/8" thick. Use gingerbread men cookie cutters to cut cookies and place on greased cookie sheet. Bake at 350°F for 10-12 minutes. Cool slightly and transfer to wire racks to finish cooling.

Drop Cookie Recipes

When you are baking, get all your ingredients out before you start the recipe. Let eggs come to room temperature. Make sure that baking powder and baking soda are fresh.

Fruity Cinnamon Cookies

2 Cups Butter

1 ½ Cups Brown Sugar

1 ½ Cups Granulated Sugar

4 Eggs

2 tsp. Vanilla Extract

5 Cups Flour

1 tsp. Cinnamon

2 tsp. Soda

2 tsp. Salt

1/3 Cup Raisins

½ Cup Dried Cranberries

Preheat oven to 375°F. Cream butter, brown sugar and granulated sugar together in a large bowl. Beat in 4 eggs (added one at a time) & vanilla. In separate bowl, mix flour, cinnamon, soda, & salt together. Stir into wet ingredients. Mix thoroughly. Add in raisins and cranberries Drop by spoonfuls onto ungreased cookie sheet. Bake for 8-10 minutes at 375˚F. For bars bake 20-25 minutes.

Spicy Cookies

2 Cups Butter

1 ½ Cups Brown Sugar

1 ½ Cups Granulated Sugar

4 Eggs

2 tsp. Vanilla

5 Cups Flour

2 tsp. Pumpkin Pie Spice

2 tsp. Soda

2 tsp. Salt

Preheat oven to 375°F. Cream butter, brown sugar and granulated sugar together in a large bowl. Beat in 4 eggs (added one at a time) & vanilla. In separate bowl, mix flour, pumpkin pie spice, soda, & salt together. Stir into wet ingredients. Mix thoroughly. Drop by spoonfuls onto ungreased cookie sheet. Bake for 8-10 minutes at 375˚F. For bars bake 20-25 minutes.

Week Three Meet with Mom

Recite Proverbs 31.

Discuss *Jesus, Fill My Heart & Home*

- List ways your home is a dwelling place.
- What are things you could do to make it more of a dwelling place?
- List ways your home is a nurturing center.
- What are things you could do or bring into your home to make it more effective as a nurturing center?

Attend a Cake Decorating Workshop or Watch a Cake Decorating Video on YouTube and decorate a cake.

Prayer Focus:

- Family Christmas

Week Three Home

Memorize Proverbs 31:10-31

Write Proverbs 31:10-31 in the version of your choice. I recommend NASB or NKJ or ESV. Then say the passage aloud.

Gardens

𝕳𝖔𝖒𝖊𝖒𝖆𝖐𝖎𝖓𝖌 is preparing and maintaining a home for those you love. It is a ministry unto the Lord and a service for your family. What a great privilege it is to create a home!

Read *The Hidden Art of Homemaking,* Chapter #6

How does God display His ability as a garden?

_____

_____

_____

Where are some of His best gardens?

_____

_____

_____

_____

𝕮𝖆𝖓 you image the first garden? It was planted by our Heavenly Father and was a joy to behold. God's garden was pleasant to look at and produced healthy vegetables, delicious fruit, and beautiful flowers. No matter how big your house or yard is, everyone can have some sort of garden, even if it is only a potted plant.

Gardens can include flowers, vines, small trees, vegetables, spices, or herbs. It is delightful to plant a garden and watch it grow. Daddy and I would plant a garden each year from seeds and we would go out each day watching to see if the seeds how sprouted yet.

I think that because we are made in the image of God and he started mankind out in a garden, it is just instinctive to want to till the soil and dig in the dirt.

Planting and nurturing a garden can also make Scriptures like John 15 and the Parable of the Sower come alive for us.

"Now the Lord God had planted a garden in the east, in Eden; and there he put the man he had formed" (Genesis 2:8 NIV ©1979).

"The LORD God took the man and put him in the Garden of Eden to work it and take care of it" (Genesis 2:15 NIV ©1979).

Who planted the first garden? Where was it located?

_____

_____

_____

What job did the Lord give Adam?

_____

_____

_____

_____

Read the following verses. Share what they teach about gardening? Any spiritual principles taught as well?

"Build houses and settle down; plant gardens and eat what they produce. Marry and have sons and daughters; find wives for your sons and give your daughters in marriage, so that they too may have sons and daughters. Increase in number there; do not decrease. Also seek the peace and prosperity of the city to which I have carried you into exile. Pray to the LORD for it, because if it prospers, you too will prosper" (Jeremiah 29:4-7 NIV ©1979).

What do these verses teach about gardening? _____

_____

_____

_____

_____

What spiritual principles are taught in this passage? _____

_____

_____

_____

_____

"He makes grass grow for the cattle, plants for man to cultivate—bringing forth food from the earth: wine that gladdens the hearts of man, oil to make his face shine, and bread that sustains the heart" (Psalm 104:14-15 NIV ©1979).

What do these verses teach about gardening? _____

_____

_____

What spiritual principles are taught in this passage? _____

_____

_____

_____

_____

"Sow your seed in the morning and in the evening let not your hands be idle, for you do not know which will succeed, *whether this or that, or whether both will do equally well"* (Ecclesiastes 11:6 NIV ©1979)

What does this verse teach about gardening? _____

_____

_____

_____

What spiritual principles are taught in this passage? _____

_____

_____

_____

_____

What are the benefits of gardening? _____

_____

_____

_____

_____

Why do you think gardening is so relaxing and/or fulfilling? _____

_____

_____

_____

_____

Gardening can be a schoolhouse for the Holy Spirit to teach us about His Truth.

What things does God teach in His Word that are illustrated with gardens or gardening?

_____

_____

_____

_____

_____

Here are some avenues for creativity in our backyard.

- Designing lawn and garden
- Caring for lawn and shrubs
- Flower gardening
- Vegetable gardening
- Herb gardening
- House plants

Get Ready to Sew a Dress

This week you will start sewing a dress. You will go to the fabric store and pick out material, a pattern, and anything you need such as thread, snaps, or zippers.

You will spend the rest of the course working on your dress. Set aside several hours twice month and you will make steady progress.

Choose a Pattern

If you have never sewn before, choose an easy-to-sew pattern. If you follow the pattern step-by-step, it will be an easy project.

Choose Material

Make sure that you like the color and style. Also, make sure that the fabric is suitable for the pattern.

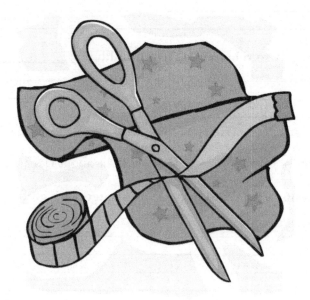

Building Her House Well Book Review

By Alice Reynolds Flower

How can a homemaker be her husband's helpmeet?

_____
_____
_____
_____
_____

How does Alice contrast homemaking & housekeeping?

_____
_____
_____

How can you build family unity?

_____
_____
_____
_____

What are the ten reasons for family worship?

_____
_____
_____
_____
_____
_____
_____
_____
_____
_____
_____
_____
_____
_____
_____
_____
_____

_____
_____
_____
_____
_____

How can we show hospitality that honors Christ?

_____
_____
_____
_____
_____

How are lean days valuable?

_____
_____
_____
_____
_____

Describe ways a wise woman can use her tongue to build?

_____
_____
_____
_____

How can a homemaker comfort others/

_____
_____
_____
_____

January: Festive & Beautiful

Memorize Proverbs 31

Jesus, Fill My Heart & Home Bible Study

Hidden Art of Homemaking

Still Life

Candy Making

Card & Gift Project

Optional: *All the The Way Home* Book Review

(Meet with Mom weekly)

Week One Meet with Mom

Recite Proverbs 31.

Discuss *Hidden Art of Homemaking*

- Describe God as a Gardener.
- Why is gardening so important?
- Why do you think people enjoy gardening?

Start Seedlings for a Spring Garden or Start an Herb Garden for the Kitchen Window

Plan a Garden together

Cut Out Your Dress

You might want to plan some weekly or monthly "All Day Sewing" workshop so you can start sewing your dress.

Prayer Focus:

- Dad

Week One Home

Memorize Proverbs 31:10-31

Write Proverbs 31:10-31 in the version of your choice. I recommend NASB or NKJ or ESV. Then say the passage aloud.

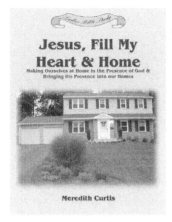

Jesus, Fill My Heart & Home Lesson 11

"Jesus Invites Himself Over"

Read and Answer Questions

How to Arrange Flowers 101

Arranging flowers is an art that adds a splash of color and beauty to any room in your house.

Thank About Where You Will Put the Arrangement

Before you begin, think about where the flower arrangement will be. Is it the dining room table? Is it a dark hallway? Is it a boring bathroom counter?

Keep the location in mind as you choose the flowers, colors, and container.

Choose a Container

When you are arranging flowers, you have to start with a vase or container.

A long thin vase works for delicate, thin stemmed flowers like lilies or a single rose.

Short, wide vases are best for large-headed, shorter-stemmed flowers like chrysanthemums.

The sky is the limit when it comes to containers. Try using egg cups, bottles, bowls, old boots, umbrella stands, teacups, or mason jars.

Choose Colors

Use colors that look good together, but don't limit yourself. Be creative. Sometimes colors combinations that shouldn't work end up looking great.

You can use colors that are next to each other on the color wheels like pink and purples or red and orange. Add a splash of a different color to add interest.

You can also make an arrangement out of different shades of the same color.

You might also do an arrangement in several different colors.

Add Texture

Add interest with texture by adding greenery, long grasses, corn stalks, or baby's breath. For seasonal flower arrangements, you can use pine cones, pumpkins, fruits, vegetables, or holly berries.

Gather the Materials You Need

Here are the materials you need to have on your work space.

- Clean Container (vase, bowl, basket)
- Floral Foam
- Floral Tape or Elastic Bands (to hold flowers together)
- A Sharp Knife or Sharp Scissors (to cut flower stems)
- Preservative Solution
- Newspaper (to cover workspace)
- The Flowers & Greenery for Arrangement

Cut Stems & Strip the Leaves

Cut at least a small amount of the stems off at the bottom. Cut diagonally about an inch. This will help the flowers absorb water.

Don't use dull scissors like kitchen scissors because dull scissors will crack the stems.

Cut off any leaves from stems that will be below the water level once the flowers are in the water.

Prepare the Vase or Container

Prepare the container by cleaning it. Make sure there is no soap residue or dirt left.

If you are using foam, let it soak in the preservation solution for 20 minutes. Cut the foam to fit into the container.

If you are using a vase without foam, add water to the bottom of the vase and mix in preservative solution.

Put the Arrangement Together

Add the larger, dominant flowers first.

Work with a singer kind of flower at a time so you can layer varieties, creating a more balanced arrangement.

Work in a circle, adding flowers around the outer edge of vase or container. Turn the container as you work, to make sure it's balanced.

Layer the flowers as you go, when you finish with one flower, add another kind of flower.

Use an odd number of flowers in each layer. This helps the arrangement look natural.

Your arrangement should 1 ½ times the height of the vase or container.

The width of the arrangement should be wide enough to add balance.

Rotate the arrangement as you work to check the height and width.

Add Leaves, Greenery, & Other Decorations

After the flowers are arranged, add in leaves, greenery, and decorations.

Fill in the spaces between flowers.

Candy Making 101

We are going to make some simple candies, starting with lollipops. If you want to move on to more complicated candies, check out a candy cookbook from the library and start cooking.

Lollipops

12 Lollipop Sticks

1 Cup Sugar

½ Cup Water

2 Tbsp. Light Corn Syrup

4-8 Drops Food Coloring of Your Choice*

2-3 Drops Flavoring Oil of Your Choice*

Line a large baking sheet with foil and lay lollipop sticks out, spacing them four inches apart.

Combine sugar, water, and corn syrup in a heavy pan over medium heat, stirring until sugar dissolves. Increase temperature to high, cover, and boil for one minute. Remove cover and boil until syrup is 310°F on a candy thermometer. Remove pan from heat and set on a wire rack.

Let the syrup cool for 5 minutes. Add food coloring and flavoring at the same time. Stir until the color is spread out evenly.

Spoon the pretty syrup over one end of each lollipop stick, making a little puddle two to three inches across. Keep them on the pan until they are completely cool and hard. Wrap each lollipop in plastic wrap and secure with a pretty ribbon below the candy.

*Choose your flavor and color to go together. For example, red will go nicely with cinnamon or cherry.

Fruit Jellies

5 ¼ oz. Packets Unflavored Gelatin

1 Cup Water

¾ Cups Strained Fresh Orange Juice or Raspberry Puree

½ Cup Superfine Sugar, plus more for serving

Line a loaf pan with foil. Oil the foil.

Pour 1 cup of water into a bowl and add gelatin. Stir to dissolve and let sit for 5 minutes.

Heat juice and 1 cup sugar until sugar is dissolved. Add softened gelatin and stir until dissolved. Pour mixture into foil-lined loaf pan and let sit at room temperature or in refrigerator until firm, about 1 hour.

Unmold the fruity gelatin slab onto a cutting board. Cut with cookie cutters or use a large sharp knife to cut into small pieces. Roll in sugar just before serving.

Homemade Peanut Butter Cups

1 Cup Creamy Peanut Butter, divided

½ Cup Confectioner's Sugar

4 ½ tsp. Butter, softened

½ tsp. Salt

2 Cups Semisweet Chocolate Chips

4 Milk Chocolate Bars, coarsely chopped

Miniature Paper Muffin Cups

Mix ½ peanut butter, confectioner's sugar, butter, and salt together until smooth.

Melt chocolate chips, candy bar pieces, and peanut butter over a double-boiler, stirring until smooth.

Drop a spoonful of chocolate mixture into each paper muffin cup. Top with a spoonful of peanut mixture. Add one more spoonful of chocolate mixture for the final layer.

Refrigerate until set. Stir in an airtight container. Enjoy!

Week Two Meet with Mom

Recite Proverbs 31.

Talk about Flower Arranging. Try making some arrangements out of silk flowers.

Make Candy Together.

Prayer Focus:

- People who need encouragement

Ministry

Think about the people you prayed for. Would they enjoy a flower arrangement or some homemade candy?

Week Two Home

Memorize Proverbs 31:10-31

Write Proverbs 31:10-31 in the version of your choice. I recommend NASB or NKJ or ESV. Then say the passage aloud.

Flower Arranging & Still Life

𝕳𝕠𝕞𝕖𝕞𝕒𝕜𝕚𝕟𝕘 is preparing and maintaining a home for those you love. It is a ministry unto the Lord and a service for your family. What a great privilege it is to create a home!

Read *The Hidden Art of Homemaking,* Chapter #7

How does God display His ability as Florist?

_____
_____
_____
_____

Where are some of His best floral arrangements?

_____
_____
_____

𝕰𝖛𝖊𝖗𝖞𝖔𝖓𝖊 can express their creativity with flowers, and every home could use some sort of flower arrangement in it. In Holland, fresh cut flowers are considered a necessity, whether rich or poor. One of the least time-consuming forms of artistic expression is to make an arrangement as a table centerpiece. The arrangement does not necessarily have to be of flowers, it can be of anything.

Centerpieces can be made of shells, fruit, vegetables, gourds, silk flowers, real flowers, candles, driftwood, stones, leaves, marbles, photographs, ornaments, or knick-knacks.

Everyone appreciates flowers. If you are helping take care of a sick person you can add a flower to their food tray. Creativity is God's gift to us and he even gives us raw materials that we can use to make out world beautiful.

My daughters fix breakfast in bed for the birthday person. They get out a pretty tray, pick a rose from outside, put it in a pretty vase, and add the rose to the platter full of delicious food. A flower on the tray adds a touch of elegance and love.

A still life is beautiful not only because of the individual parts but because of how they blend together in a setting. Flower arranging is a still life made of flowers.

What are some places in you homes where you have still lifes?

_____
_____
_____

What does a centerpiece on the table communicate?

_____
_____
_____
_____
_____
_____
_____
_____

Dresser tops, shelves, and table tops are all the perfect places for still lifes. It is so fun to create a Christmas still life for the holidays.

A dining room table can become a medium for beauty and art. A bright birthday tablecloth, matching napkins, and bright candles in a candelabra communicates to everyone that someone is having a birthday party and it's time to celebrate!

What fun the next time you make tacos to decorate the table Mexican style.

Here are some still lifes that we have done. You will make two of your own.

Choosing the Perfect Gift

When Christmas and birthdays come around, it's gift giving time. Do you enjoy getting gifts or do you have trouble picking out the right gift?

Here are some tips for picking out the perfect gift.

Think about things the person needs or likes. How about hobbies? Interests? Favorite colors? Favorite sports teams? Favorite books? Favorite music?

Does he or she have a wish lists?

Choose one person: _____

List gift ideas: _____   _____

_____   _____   _____

_____   _____   _____

Week Three Meet with Mom

Recite Proverbs 31.

Create your own still life. Orseveral. It might be a dinner table centerpiece, dresser top, kitchen countertop, end table, coffee table, or welcome table at church.

You might do more flower arranging, too.

Prayer Focus:

- Prayer Life

Week Three Home

Memorize Proverbs 31:10-31

Write Proverbs 31:10-31 in the version of your choice. I recommend NASB or NKJ or ESV. Then say the passage aloud.

Food

Homemaking is preparing and maintaining a home for those you love. It is a ministry unto the Lord and a service for your family. What a great privilege it is to create a home!

Read *The Hidden Art of Homemaking,* Chapter #8

How does God display His ability as a Chef?

_____
_____
_____
_____

What kind of food has He provided for us?

_____
_____
_____
_____

When we lived in Virginia, I loved to bake bread every week. I loved punching down the dough and letting it rise. When it was chilly in the winter months, I would bake bread on laundry day and let it rise on the warm dryer.

What is so wonderful about freshly baked bread? I love the smell, but I also loved the kneading. I don't enjoy making bread in a bread machine because I miss kneading the bread.

It is our privilege and responsibility to provide delicious, nutritious meals for our families.

"She is like the merchant ships, bringing her food from afar. She gets up while it is still dark, she provides food for her family and portions for her servant girls" (Proverbs 31:14-15 NIV ©1979).

What are merchant ships like? _____
_____
_____
_____

How are we to be like merchant ships? _____
_____
_____
_____
_____

Providing food for our families is a wife's responsibility. We have the privilege of shopping, bargain hunting, and finding what will delight our families at mealtime.

Homemakers can tell one another about sales and share recipes. I enjoy planning menus and shopping lists. To save money, you must plan your meals ahead so that you can look for bargains and sales. I would plan my menus the day the sale papers came out. That way I could plan meals around the sale items.

If your life is busy like mine, try making extra and freezing meals for busy days. When I cook chicken, I like to cook extra, cube it, and freeze it for casseroles.

A plate of food should be a still life. When you are preparing a meal, think of color, texture, flavor, and smell. As an artist, you are blending these things together to make something beautiful, nutritious, and edible.

Our family loves traditional food for holidays and special occasions. We always let the birthday person pick out the menu on their special day.

"Here I am! I stand at the door and knock. If anyone hears my voice and opens the door, I will come in and eat with him and he with me" (Revelation 3:20 NIV ©1979).

Eat in an atmosphere of communion and intimacy. Family mealtimes should be peaceful and joyful. My grandmother would not allow any negative talk at the dinner table. "It ruins digestion," she would say. If she had caught the kitchen on fire while Grandpa was at work, she would just wait to tell him after dinner.

Jesus can be part of our mealtimes. How can Jesus be part of our family mealtimes?

_____
_____
_____
_____
_____
_____

"All the days of the oppressed are wretched, but the cheerful heart has a continual feast. Better a little with the fear of the LORD than great wealth with turmoil. Better a meal of vegetables where there is love, than a fattened calf with hatred" (Proverbs 15:15-17 NIV ©1979).

What is contrasted here?

_____
_____
_____
_____
_____

What is true wealth?

_____
_____
_____
_____
_____

How can love rule and reign at family mealtimes?

_____
_____
_____
_____
_____
_____
_____

"The purposes of a man's heart are deep waters, but a man of understanding draws them out" (Proverbs 20:5 NIV ©1979).

Applying this verse to our children, how can we be wives and mothers of understanding?

_____
_____
_____
_____
_____

What beats in your husband's heart? His dreams? Failures? Successes? Trials? And what beats in your children's heart? Here are some questions you can ask.

- "What is your favorite character in the book you are reading?"
- "What was the highlight of your day?"
- "On a scale of 1 to 10, how would you rate your day?"

Hospitality

If Jesus called you on the phone and said that He was coming over for dinner in three days and you should invite five guests to join Him and your family, who would you invite?

_____
_____
_____
_____
_____

The Bible has a lot to say about hospitality. Read the following verses and think about how hospitality plays into each one.

"Those who accepted his message were baptized, and about three thousand were added to their number that day. They devoted themselves to the apostles teaching and to the fellowship, to the breaking of bread and to prayer. Everyone was filled with awe, and many miraculous signs were done by the apostles. All the believers were together and had everything in common. Selling their possessions and goods, they gave to anyone as he had need. Every day they continued to meet together in the temple courts. They broke bread together in their homes and ate together with glad and sincere hearts, praising God and enjoying the favor of all the people" (Acts 2:41-47 NIV ©1979)

"Offer hospitality to one another without grumbling" (I Peter 4:9 NIV ©1979).

"Share with God's people who are in need. Practice hospitality" (Romans 12:13 NIV ©1979).

"Do not forget to entertain strangers, for by so doing some have entertained angels without knowing it" (Hebrews 13:2 NIV).

"Then Jesus said to His host, "When you give a luncheon or dinner, do not invite your friends, your brothers or relatives, or your rich neighbors; if you do, they may invite you back and so you will be repaid. But when you give a banquet, invite the poor, the crippled, the lame, the blind, and you will be blessed. Although they cannot repay you, you will be repaid at the resurrection of the righteous" (Luke 14:12-14 NIV ©1979).

Here are some hints and tips to make hospitality a joy!

1. Pray for guests before they arrive.
2. Be real.
3. Let your family and house be real.
4. Let the meal be simple enough so that you can focus on the guests.
5. Be creative & daring when you feel like it. But don't make every hospitality endeavor an event or you will burn out. Sometimes china and sometimes paper plates.
6. Prepare ahead of time, if possible.
7. Spontaneous can be the most fun.

How to Bake Bread the Old-Fashioned Way

Yes, I know your family probably has a stand mixer with a dough hook and a bread machine, but I want you to, at least once in your life, make bread the old-fashioned way.

You will need to remove your rings to do this.

It's time to mix the dough with a wooden spoon, knead the dough yourself, and let it rise in a heavy bowl with a kitchen towel draped across it. There is something relaxing and soothing about kneading dough with your hands.

Bread Recipes

Here are some bread recipes that I've made since the early days of my marriage. They are easy to make and taste delicious.

Oatmeal Bread

1 Cup Uncooked Oatmeal

½ Cup Molasses

2 Tbsp. Oil

1/2 tsp. salt

2 Cups Boiling Water

5 Cups Flour

1 pkg. Dry Yeast

Mix together the uncooked oatmeal, molasses, shorting, and salt. Cover with boiling water and let set for 5 minutes. Add the flour and dry yeast, mix well. Let rise about 1 hour and 15 minutes. Shape into 2 loaves and let rise again for 1 hour and 15 minutes. Bake at 375°F for 25 to 30 minutes. While still hot rub top with margarine or butter.

Whole Wheat Bread

6-7 Cups Whole Wheat Flour

2 Tbsp. Butter

2 Packages Dry Yeast

2 ½ Cups Hot (not boiling) Water

1/3 Cup Honey

Vegetable Oil (to brush surface)

In a large bowl stir 2 cups flour, dry yeast, and salt. Add honey and butter. Pour hot water over all and beat with electric mixer 2 minutes at medium speed. Add 1 ½ cups more flour and continue beating until thick and elastic. With a wooden spoon, stir in two more cups of flour. Gradually add remaining flour until a soft dough is formed. Knead 5-10 minutes. Cover and let rest 20 minutes. Punch and divide. Place in greased pans. Brush surface with oil, cover with towels and refrigerate. Wait 5-6 hours [up to 24 hours]. Let stand 10 minutes before baking. Bake at 400°F for 35-40 minutes.

White Bread

1 Package Dry Yeast

½ Cup Butter

1 Cup Water

2 tsp. Salt

2 Cups Milk, scalded

7 ½ - 8 Cups Flour

½ Cup Sugar

2 Eggs

Soften dry yeast in water. Pour scalded milk over sugar and butter and salt, stirring to dissolve. Cool to lukewarm. Add 3 cups flour and mix well.

Stir in eggs and yeast mixture. Add the rest of flour to make a soft dough. Knead 8-10 minutes. Put in buttered bowl and let rise 1½-2 hours. Punch dough and divide dough in half. Let rest 10 minutes.

Divide dough into 2 loaf pans. Bake 375°F until lightly brown.

Timeless Treasures Book Review

By Mary Pride

Describe the author. What is her worldview? What is her personality like? How does it come through in her writing?

_____

_____

_____

What does Emilie say that our timeless treasures symbolize?

_____

_____

_____

Go on a room-by-room treasure hunt. What treasures do you find in your house?

_____

_____

_____

_____

_____

Have you ever been exploring in an attic? What treasures did you find?

_____

_____

_____

What treasures would you like to keep in your house one day?

_____

_____

_____

Have you ever made something for someone that is a treasure to them? What is it?

_____

_____

_____

February: Nutrition & Food

Memorize Proverbs 31

Jesus, Fill My Heart & Home Bible Study

Hidden Art of Homemaking

Nutrition

Make Jam

Poetry

Optional: *The Stay at Home Mom* Book Review

(Meet with Mom weekly)

Week One Meet with Mom

Recite Proverbs 31.

Discuss *Hidden Art of Homemaking*

- Discuss Artistry in Food.

Make St. Valentine's Day Cards

Prayer Focus:

- Prayer Life

Week One Home

Memorize Proverbs 31:10-31

Write Proverbs 31:10-31 in the version of your choice. I recommend NASB or NKJ or ESV. Then say the passage aloud.

Nutrition 101

Nutrition: Water & A Balanced Diet

People disagree on what makes a healthy diet, but most people agree that our body needs certain nutrients to function efficiently. Let's take a look at those nutrients.

- Water
- Fiber
- Carbohydrates
- Fats
- Proteins
- Vitamins
- Minerals

We will talk about Water and Homeostasis first. Then we will talk briefly about the other nutrients our body needs.

Homeostasis

I remember working in a hospital on a surgical floor. My patients would check in to have surgery. It was like a little world. There were so many different places to explore and so many different people to meet. My friend Tony was a lab technician who drew people's blood on my surgical floor and worked in the lab on the first floor. Susie was a respiratory therapist who would travel from floor to floor to give respiratory treatments to patients, but her office was on the third floor. The surgeons came before and after surgery to check on the patients, but they spent most of their time in the operating room where it was very cold. I only saw the recovery room nurses when they returned the patients to my floor. I never even saw the recovery room. Me? Well, I worked on the fourth-floor surgical unit getting patients ready for surgery and taking care of them afterward. There were so many people involved in my patient's experience and it was very important that everyone knew what they were doing, where they needed to be, and communicated with each other. Otherwise, the patient might not have come out of the surgery alive!

Your body is like that too. It is doing so many things just to keep you alive. Your body takes in air, harvests oxygen, digests food, sends glucose to the cells for energy, excretes waste products through urine, keeps your heart beating, and regulates a constant temperature. There are so many things you don't even think about! At the same time, it helps you to think, run, and make things.

Your body is constantly busy. There are so many different processes going on at the same time. Yet, with all the busyness, your body must maintain a perfect balance at all times of oxygen levels, carbon dioxide levels, hormone rations, and heart rate rhythms. Your body must stay at a constant temperature, meet hunger needs, and inform the body when it needs to drink more water. So many body processes require a delicate balance to work efficiently (homeostatis). Our bodies are just amazing!

Jay Wile says, in *The Human Body: Fearfully and Wonderfully Made*, "Homeostasis is a state of equilibrium in the body with respect to its functions, chemical levels, and tissues." (Page 5)

Homeostasis is the work of keeping your internal environment concentrations and measurements within a narrow range. Homeostasis is the process of maintaining a stable internal balance in your body. Many things in our body have set points that have to be maintained. Our temperature must be maintained inside our body at a set point. Glucose levels and oxygen levels must be at a certain concentration in the blood. There is a constant battle inside the body to keep these levels stable.

The hypothalamus plays a big role in this balance regulation. The hypothalamus is a part of the brain located in just above the brain stem and is a group of neurons. This group of neurons called the hypothalamus forms the most important link between the nervous system and the endocrine system. The hypothalamus is responsible for regulating temperature, thirst, hunger, blood pressure, and heart rhythms.

The kidneys also play an important role in homeostasis. They regulate the amount of water in the body and keep the concentration of mineral ions to acceptable levels in your blood. In fact, one way a doctor can tell if someone is wrong with your health is to examine your blood to measure the different concentrations. If those numbers are out of whack, something is wrong. The kidneys also get rid of waste products and toxins, while holding on to glucose and proteins. Another way to tell is something is wrong with your health is to measure the concentration of glucose and protein in your blood.

Why Our Body Needs Water

Our bodies are almost three-fourths water. Water plays an important role in our bodies. We need just the right amount of fluid inside and outside each cell. This fluid balance is important to stay healthy.

Water is a solvent. That means that other substances can be dissolved in water. Water can be used to carry nutrients, oxygen, salivary amylase, and blood cells. Water is used in food digestion to help move the food along and to allow nutrients to dissolve so they can pass through the intestinal walls into the bloodstream. Water carries toxic waste outside of your body (urine, sweat). Water is a medium where biochemical, metabolic reactions can occur. Water helps to regulate body temperature. Water is mixed with other things to act as a lubricant for our moving parts. Water also provides a moist environment for your mouth and nose.

There is water inside your cells. In this fluid, the parts of a cell live and work. If there is not enough water inside a cell, the cell shrivels and dies. If there is too much water inside a cell, the cell will burst.

How to Get the Water Our Body Needs

Healthy people meet their need for water by eating food with water inside and drinking when they are thirsty. Some foods are mostly water like celery, watermelon, oranges, and melons. Soups and broths have a lot of water too.

All liquid beverages have water in them and count as water intake, however, beverages with caffeine also act as a diuretic. A diuretic cause you to get rid of water in your bloodstream through the kidneys and urine. So, if you drink a cup of coffee you are getting water, but still causing your body to get rid of water—defeating the purpose! Other beverages often contain sugar or other ingredients that can add empty calories to your diet. Drinking fruit juice gives your body water, but you lose the bulk, or fiber, of the fruit, so use fruit juices instead of water sparingly. Sodas and other sugary beverages allow us to consume massive amounts of sugar without realizing it. So, as much as you can, drink lots of plain old water!

However, if the weather is hot or you are exercising, you will need more water. You also need more water if you have a fever or diarrhea. In these situations, it is important to eat before you feel hungry.

When you live in a hot, humid place like I do in Central Florida, it is a good idea to drink as much water as you can. I often have a glass of water close by so that whenever I am thirsty, I can take a drink. It is easy to get dehydrated in Florida and not know it.

There is not a simple formula for how much water people need to drink. How much water you need each day depends on your age, weight, physical exertion, and overall health. Some people say you should get all your water through your food while others say you should drink 1-2 gallons of water a day.

The best way to tell if you are drinking enough water is not counting glasses. I think the best way to tell if you are getting enough water is to look at your urine. If your urine is a bright yellow or brown color, you need to drink more water. Your urine should be a very pale yellow color and you should urinate several times a day.

Dehydration

Tommy stopped the lawn mower and wiped the sweat off his forehead. He was feeling queasy. He wondered if he was getting the flu. His mouth felt dry and his head hurt. Suddenly he felt so dizzy that he knew he better sit down. What is wrong with Tommy?

Tommy is dehydrated. He has not drinking enough water, sweating, and working in the hot sun has worked together to put his body in a situation where it doesn't have enough water to carry out its normal jobs. Mild dehydration can be treated by drinking water, but severe dehydration will require medical care. Yes, it's that serious!

How can someone tell if they are dehydrated? The symptoms are thirst (of course!), exhaustion, dry mouth, dry skin, headache, dizziness, constipation, and dark yellow urine or no urine at all. If someone has severe dehydration, they will have a rapid heartbeat, rapid breathing, low blood pressure, sunken eyes, and fever. A severely dehydrated person will be grumpy and sometimes confused. They might even be delirious if dehydration gets too serious. In severe cases of dehydration, you can have seizures, swelling of the brain, or kidney failure.

What causes dehydration? In Tommy's case, it was a combination of not drinking enough water, heat, and exercise. Other causes can be high fevers, diarrhea, or vomiting because the body loses water in these conditions.

Can Our Bodies Get Too Much Water?

"I'll take that in. I'm giving Paul his meds," I said, taking a lunch tray from the nurse's aide who was about to walk into Paul's room. Paul was a quadriplegic and often in and out of the hospital for surgery.

"Hi, Paul," I greeted him, setting the tray down on his bedside table.

"Duck nursie!" He yelled. "There's a monkey on your head. Look they're everywhere! See the monkeys!"

Quickly scanning the room, I realized at once there were no monkeys. But, I realized that Paul had consumed too much water. He was experiencing hyponatremia, or low concentration levels of sodium. Remember I told you that are bodies have to maintain a delicate balance of mineral ions in the bloodstream? Well, Paul had consumed so much water that he had diluted the mineral content in his blood. His kidneys were not able to work fast enough to get rid of the extra water.

You see, Paul was a quadriplegic and, as a quadriplegic, very susceptible to urinary tract infections. Paul was advised to drink lot of water, but Paul took it to an extreme. Paul drank almost several gallons of water—so much water that his kidneys couldn't keep up.

This is rare in our nation. Most Americans really don't drink enough water.

Nutrition: A Balanced Diet

Diet is the foods you eat all the time. If you normally eat cereal for breakfast, a sandwich for lunch, and meat and salad for dinner, that is a typical diet. We are going to talk about how to eat a healthy diet.

How to Eat a Balanced Diet

Let's talk about some principles that will help you eat a balanced diet.

Let's start with some biblical principles of food and eating. Look up the verse and write it out on the lines below.

We eat to the glory of God (I Corinthians 10:31) _____

_____

_____

He gave us all things for us to richly enjoy, including food (I Timothy 6:17b) _____

_____

_____

All things are permissible, but not all things are beneficial (I Corinthians 10:23) _____

_____

_____

God declared all foods clean—we are not under the Law in our diet! (Mark 7:18-19) _____
_____
_____
_____
_____

It is not good to eat too much honey (Proverbs 25:27) _____
_____
_____

Gluttony is to be avoided! (Proverbs 23:1-2) _____
_____
_____
_____

We are warned not to fall into legalism (Colossians 2:20-22) Summarize please. _____
_____
_____

As you can, see the God wants us to enjoy food, but use self-control in how much food we eat. God made our bodies and He knows what is best for them. Sometimes a food plan that works for someone else doesn't work for you. God cares what we eat and wants eating to be a pleasure, not a drudgery or an experience of worshipping food!

Eat meals that have a wide variety of colors, textures, and shapes. Orange vegetables are often high in vitamin A. Think color when you think of fruits and vegetables—eat a wide variety of colors! Whole grain bread has a lot more texture to it than squishy white bread. I like to think of my plate as a piece of art. Eat food with texture. I want it to be lovely to look at and lovely to taste.

Eat food that is as close to its natural state as possible. Green beans from the back-yard garden are better to eat than green beans from a can. Meat without hormones and antibiotics added is healthier than meat with those things. Avoid foods that are prepared ahead and packaged. Learn to read labels. If you aren't sure what an ingredient is, don't eat the food.

Get your vitamins and minerals in your food. Think about nutrients and eating foods with those nutrients. This might cause you to try new foods.

Listen to your body. Sometimes we eat when we are really thirsty. Sometimes we eat what's in front of our eyes, instead of figuring out what we are hungry for. If I am crazing chocolate ice cream, maybe I am really craving calcium or iron.

Make healthy choices. When you want something sweet, eat a piece of fruit instead of a piece of cake. Eat unhealthy foods in moderation. If you deprive yourself completely, they will become a longing. Consider sticking to a healthy eating plan six days and week and on the seventh day, eat whatever you want to.

Food can be used to heal our bodies. Garlic and onions work as natural antibiotics. Ginger and peppermint can settle our stomachs. Fiber can help us overcome constipation. Always try a natural remedy before popping a pill. And, of course, eating a balanced, healthy diet will help our bodies stay in tip-top shape.

Balanced Diet

So, what is a balanced diet? I'm glad you asked. A balanced diet is made up of macronutrients like fats, carbohydrates, and proteins which give energy to our body. We can calculate that energy in terms of calories. In addition, our bodies need vitamins and minerals.

Foods can be rich in carbohydrates or a good source of vitamin A, but they have other ingredients too. For instance, a carrot has carbohydrates and vitamin A. There is no protein, fat, or calcium in carrots, but there is a tiny bit of vitamin C and iron.

Here's another example. Pretend that you are eating a chicken breast with nothing on it. The chicken breast has protein, fat and B vitamins with a little bit of sodium. There is also a tiny bit of calcium, vitamin A, and iron.

Calories

We hear about calories all the time. If we eat a low-calorie diet, we will lose weight. But what is a calorie? A calorie is a measurement of energy. Just as we measure things in inches or cups or tablespoons, we measure energy for our body in calories.

A calorie is the energy it takes to raise 1 gram of water 1 degree Celsius. Our bodies need calories, or energy, to digest food, breathe in and out, and keep our heart beating. On the laziest of lazy days our bodies need 1,000 to 1,400 calories just to keep the heart beating and everything else working. If you are more active, you would need to add at least 600 more calories to your fuel intake.

If you get more calories of energy than your body needs, it stores the extra energy as fat.

For every gram of protein, there are 4 calories of energy. For every gram of carbohydrates, there are 4 calories of energy. But, fat, is the best provider of calories, with 9 calories for every gram of fat.

Let's take a brief look at some of those vitamins and minerals our bodies need.

Fiber

Fiber helps our food pass quickly and easily through the digestive tract. No one likes to have diarrhea or constipation. Fiber prevents both! There are two kinds of fiber: soluble and insoluble. Soluble fiber fills up with water, giving bulk to our feces, or poop. Insoluble fiber passes quickly through our bodies to speed up the process of digestion. Eat both kinds of fiber for a healthy diet.

Good sources of fiber include salads, fresh fruit, fresh vegetables, oats, bran cereal, brown rice, beans, and nuts.

Carbohydrates

Carbohydrates give our bodies energy. Carbohydrates can be simple (sugar, fruit) or complex (bread, rice, potatoes). All carbohydrates are turned into glucose for the body to use for energy. Simple sugars are turned into glucose right away. Complex carbohydrates take longer for your body to absorb and turn into glucose so they help you to feel fuller and more satisfied. Some complex carbohydrates are higher in fiber, but we will talk about fiber separately. Carbohydrates contain vitamins and minerals our bodies need as well.

Healthy sources of simple carbohydrates are fresh fruit, honey, raw sugar, and molasses. Healthy sources of complex carbohydrates are bread, brown rice, popcorn, oatmeal, quinoa, barley, corn, potatoes, carrots, peas, beans, and nuts.

Fats

Our bodies need fat for energy. We get most of the fat our body needs through oil and fats. Fats are solid at room temperature and oils are liquid at room temperature. Fats, or lipids, are part of every cell in your body. They help make up the cell membrane. They insulate us and hold in heat. Fats are converted into energy, or fuel, for our bodies. Extra food energy is stored as fat in our bodies. These fat cells surround and protect our organs and provide shape to our bodies.

Olive oil, coconut oil, butter, avocados, nuts, dairy products, fish, and meat are all sources of fat.

Protein

Proteins, made up of amino acids, are important nutrients. Our bodies need them to repair muscles, tissue repair, contract muscles, transmit nerve messages, and transport nutrients. Proteins play a role in every single cell, tissue, and organ in your body. Pregnant women and growing children need lots of protein to grow stronger. Digestive Enzymes are needed to break proteins down into amino acids.

Beef, chicken, fish, lamb, turkey, eggs, dairy products, legumes, and nuts are great sources of protein.

Vitamins

Our bodies also need vitamins. Some vitamins are fat-soluble (Vitamin K, E, D, & A) and others are water-soluble (Vitamin C and the B Vitamins). Fat-soluble vitamins can be stored in your body and you can actually have toxic levels of these vitamins. Water soluble vitamins are excreted (or pass through) in your urine so you need to constantly replenish these stores.

Vitamin A

Vitamin A is an antioxidant that protects the lungs from smoke and other toxins. Vitamin A also plays a role in the immune system, reproduction, skin health, and is critical for healthy vision.

Food sources of Vitamin A include carrots, pumpkin, sweet potatoes, cod liver oil, tuna, milk, red chili peppers, red bell peppers, paprika, butternut squash, mangoes, mustard greens, dried apricots, basil, kale, cantaloupe, peas, turnip greens, tomatoes, spinach, papaya, iceberg lettuce, and romaine lettuce.

Vitamin D

Vitamin D is fat-soluble vitamin necessary for strong bones, teeth, muscles, and lungs. Vitamin D, an antioxidant protects cells from oxidation damage. Vitamin D helps the body absorb calcium, phosphorus, and other important minerals. Here's the cool thing—your body makes its own Vitamin D if you get enough sunlight. Yes, it's true!

It's very hard to get Vitamin D from food. You get Vitamin D from sunlight or supplements. But, there are several foods that are fortified with Vitamin D. That means that Vitamin D is added. Milk and cereals often have Vitamin D added. Fatty fish like tuna and salmon, cod liver oil do contain Vitamin D. Liver, cheese, and egg yolks also contain very small amounts of Vitamin D.

When you wear sunscreen, it blocks Vitamin D exposure. Clouds, air pollution, and glass all bock the rays you need for Vitamin D production. The more skin exposed, the more Vitamin D your body can make. Now, hold on, I'm not encouraging you to run around naked outside. You don't need large amounts of sun exposure, especially here in Florida. A walk around the block each day in a short-sleeved shirt will give your body all the sunshine it needs to make Vitamin D.

Vitamin E

Vitamin E is a fat-soluble vitamin that can be stored in your body. Vitamin E, an anti-oxidant protects cell membranes and tissues from oxidation damage, helps create red blood cells, aids the body in using vitamin K, slows down the aging process, and plays a role in healthy cholesterol levels.

Shrimp, fish, avocados, olives, olive oil, vegetable oils, peanut butter, tomatoes, carrots, kiwifruit, cranberries, collard greens, spinach, almonds, turnip greens, Swiss chard, beet greens, asparagus, broccoli, sunflower seeds, and nuts are great sources of Vitamin E.

Vitamin K

Vitamin K is a fat-soluble vitamin best known for helping with blood clotting. But, Vitamin K also protects the heart, helps to build strong bones, and helps to regulate insulin levels.

Vitamin K can be found in lamb, duck, dark turkey meat, dark chicken meat, liver, beef, eggs, kale, spinach, turnip greens, collards, Swiss chard, cabbage, Brussels sprouts, and cauliflower.

Vitamin C

Vitamin C is an antioxidant and water-soluble so cannot be stored in body, must get new supply each day. Vitamin C fights free radicals, prevents scurvy, supports the immune system, aids in blood clotting, and supports healthy skin. Vitamin C is part of the collagen-making process. Collagen gives support to tendons, ligaments, bones, and blood vessels. We think of vitamin C as a cold-preventer. Helps enhance body's absorption of iron.

Tomatoes, bell peppers, potatoes, broccoli, oranges, grapefruit, lemons, tangerines, papayas, strawberries, pineapple, kiwifruit, cantaloupe, mango, guavas, kale, and chili peppers are great sources of Vitamin C.

Vitamin B Complex Vitamins

All vitamin B vitamins play a role in metabolism of carbohydrate, fat, and protein to give the body energy, contribute to red blood cell production, and help maintain healthy skin, hair, eyes, liver, and nervous system.

Vitamin B1—Thiamin

Vitamin B1, or thiamine, is often considered the "anti-stress vitamin". It helps control the appetite and promote growth and muscle tone. Thiamine plays a key role in the metabolism of carbohydrates, fats, and proteins.

Good sources of thiamine are beef kidneys, liver, nuts, legumes, romaine lettuce, spinach, tomatoes, cabbage, black beans, brown rice, wheat germ, and whole grains.

Vitamin B2—Riboflavin

Vitamin B2, or riboflavin, helps the body metabolize carbohydrates, fats, and proteins to produce energy. Riboflavin specifically works as an antioxidant, rounding up free radicals and getting rid of them before they can damage cells. Riboflavin prevents cataracts, aids in vision, and prevents eye fatigue.

Good sources of Riboflavin are cheese, chicken, turkey, fish, milk, yogurt, cheese, spinach, and wheat germ.

Vitamin B3—Niacin

Vitamin B3, or Niacin, stays busy removing toxic chemicals from the body as an antioxidant. It helps make sex hormones and stress-related hormones in the adrenal glands. It improves circulation and reduces cholesterol levels. Niacin supports the central nervous system.

Good sources of Niacin are chicken, pork, turkey, sardines, tuna, green peas, broccoli, and peanuts.

Vitamin B5—Pantothenic Acid)

Pantothenic Acid, or vitamin B5, helps manufacture sex hormones and stress hormones in the adrenal glands. It also helps synthesize cholesterol. Pantothenic Acid supports the central nervous system, the gastrointestinal tract, and immune system. It helps the body use vitamins and helps build antibodies.

Good sources of Pantothenic Acid are beef, milk, eggs, broccoli, and yeast.

Vitamin B6—Pyridoxine

Pyridoxine, or vitamin B6 helps build DNA, RNA, and antibodies. It helps build neurotransmitters and regulate sodium and phosphorus in body. Pyridoxine promotes healthy skin and reduces cramps, stiffness, and numbness.

Good sources of Pyridoxine are beef liver, tuna, potatoes, beans, rice, wheat germ, bananas, and avocado.

Vitamin B7—Vitamin H—Biotin

Biotin, Vitamin H, or Vitamin B7, promotes healthy nails, hair, and skin. It helps the body use the other B vitamins and reduces blood sugar levels. Good sources of biotin are beef, milk, eggs, broccoli, and yeast.

Vitamin B9—Folic Acid

Folic Acid, or vitamin B9, helps make DNA, RNA, and red blood cells. It also aids in amino acid metabolism and helps iron function in the body. It brings mental and emotional health.

Good sources of folic acid are liver, beans, wheat bran, citrus fruit, beans, bananas, apples, eggs, avocado, coffee, rice, and blueberries.

Menu Planning

In the early years of homemaking, I made monthly menus. After I made my menus, I made my grocery list. Making monthly menus lowed the grocery bills and kept me from making last-minute runs to the grocery store.

Here are some tips on making a family menu:

- Make a list of all the dishes you cook well. You might want to search for recipes each week. Try one or two new recipes a week.
- Make a list of your family members' favorite foods.
- Think about the weather. Salads are great for the summer and soups for the winter.
- Don't forget to think about nutrition both daily and weekly. Eat a variety of foods that will provide the carbohydrates, fats, protein, water, vitamins, and minerals everyone needs.
- Write down the dishes on a calendar or planner. Make a list of dishes you want to try in the future.
- Try theme nights like Mexican Monday or Taco Tuesday.
- Plan to use leftovers for lunch the next day or have a leftover night.

Now, it's time to make a weekly menu for breakfast, lunch, and dinner for your family.

Sunday	Monday	Tuesday	Wednesday	Thursday	Friday	Saturday
Breakfast	Breakfast	Breakfast	Breakfast	Breakfast	Breakfast	Breakfast
Lunch	Lunch	Lunch	Lunch	Lunch	Lunch	Lunch
Dinner	Dinner	Dinner	Dinner	Dinner	Dinner	Dinner

Week Two Meet with Mom

Recite Proverbs 31.

Discuss Nutrition & Menu Planning

Share Menus

Prayer Focus:

- Relationships

Week Two Home

Memorize Proverbs 31:10-31

Write Proverbs 31:10-31 in the version of your choice. I recommend NASB or NKJ or ESV. Then say the passage aloud.

Writing, Prose, Poetry

𝕳𝖔𝖒𝖊𝖒𝖆𝖐𝖎𝖓𝖌 is preparing and maintaining a home for those you love. It is a ministry unto the Lord and a service for your family. What a great privilege it is to create a home!

Read *The Hidden Art of Homemaking,* Chapter #9

How does God display His ability as Writer? _____
_____
_____
_____

Where are some of His best works? _____
_____
_____
_____
_____

𝕱𝖗𝖔𝖒 what we have studied or read so far, what are you discovering are your creative strengths? What would you like help from others in?

"For the word of God is living and active. Sharper than any double-edged sword, it penetrates even to dividing soul and spirit, joints and marrow; it judges the thoughts and attitudes of the heart" (Hebrews 4:12 NIV ©1979).

"All Scripture is God-breathed and is useful for teaching, rebuking, correcting and training in righteousness, so that the man of God may be thoroughly equipped for every good work" (II Timothy 3:16 NIV ©1979).

God writes to us through His Word!

"He who was seated on the throne said, "I am making everything new!" Then he said, "Write this down for these words are trustworthy and true" (Revelation 21:5 NIV ©1979).

God wanted this written down because it was important!

Writing is communication. Prose and poetry are both art and communication. The medium is the written language. There is rhythm and balance in poetry and prose. It is singing or painting with words.

All writing, whether fiction, nonfiction, poetry, or prose, should adhere to God's standards. Communication should be concrete, concise, and gracious.

Concrete: explaining clearly and completely so as to accurately plant a picture in the reader's mind.

Concise: stated as briefly as possible without sacrificing concreteness.

Gracious: words and attitudes behind them should be kind, truthful and polite according to Ephesians 4:29.

"Do not let any unwholesome words come out of your mouth, but only what is helpful for building others up according to their needs, that it may benefit those who listen," (Ephesians 4:29 NIV).

Communication should be undertaken with wisdom whether using mouth or pen.

"Not many of you should presume to be teachers, my brothers, because you know that we who teach will be judged more strictly. We all stumble in many ways. If anyone is never at fault in what he says, he is a perfect man, able to keep his whole body in check.

"When we put bits into the mouths of horses to make them obey us, we can turn the whole animal. Or take ships as an example. Although they are so large and are driven by strong winds, they are steered by a very small rudder wherever the pilot wants to go. Likewise, the tongue is a small part of the body, but it makes great boasts. Consider what a great forest is set on fire by a small spark. The tongue also is a fire, a world of evil among the parts of the body. It corrupts the whole person, sets the whole course of his life on fire, and is itself set on fire by hell.

"All kinds of animals, birds, reptiles and creatures of the sea are being tamed and have been tamed by man, but no man can tame the tongue. It is a restless evil, full of deadly poison.

"With the tongue, we praise our Lord and Father, and with it we curse men, who have been made in God's likeness. Out of the same mouth come praise and cursing. My brothers, can a fig tree bear olives, or a grapevine bear figs? Neither can a salt spring produce fresh water.

"Who is wise and understand among you? Let him show it by his good life, by deeds done in the humility that comes from wisdom. But if you harbor bitter envy and selfish ambition in your hearts, do not boast about it or deny the truth. Such "wisdom" does not come down from heaven but is earthly, unspiritual and of the devil. For where you have envy and selfish ambition, there you find disorder and every evil practice.

"But the wisdom that comes from heaven is first of all pure; then peace-loving, considerate, submissive, full of mercy and good fruit, impartial and sincere. Peacemakers who sow in peace raise a harvest of righteousness" (James 3:1-18 NIV ©1979).

What three subjects are addressed in this passage?

_____
_____
_____

What does this passage teach about teachers?

_____
_____
_____

What does this passage teach about the tongue?

_____

_____

_____

_____

What does this passage teach about wisdom?

_____

_____

_____

How are these three subjects related?

_____

_____

_____

_____

_____

Different kinds of teachers exist in the local church with differing authority and responsibility.

- Teacher (Eph. 4 full time man)
- teachers (gift of teaching)
- Elder (must be able to teach)
- Parents (commanded to teach children)
- Older Women (commanded to teach younger women)
- Teach one another (All Christians commanded to teach and admonish one another)

After dealing with the motivation and wisdom of writing, what writing can we do?

_____

_____

_____

_____

_____

_____

Prose, poetry and literature are considered "art." Nonfiction writing can express our God-given creativity too. Here are different kinds of writing you can do.

- Writing our prayers (Psalms are prayers and songs of David and others)
- Keeping a written record of answered prayers and miracles
- Letters to families and friends (or E-mail)

- Love notes to husband and children
- Encouragement notes to others
- Write a tract of our personal testimony and making copies to hand out
- Letters to Editor
- Articles
- Short stories
- Poems

After pleasing God, the most important thing about writing is your audience. Who are they? How old? What are their interests? What is the reading level? What will bless them?

It's the same old "Eyes off self and onto Jesus and others," one of the principles of the Upside-Down Kingdom.

If you are writing an article for publication, you need to ask some more questions. What is editor looking for? Read several copies of magazine. When you write an article, target the magazine and magazine audience. If you want to become a writer, don't read books on writing. Just Write! Write! Write!

How to Make Jam

Making jam is easy and fun. Best of all, it tastes delicious. All you have to do is by a package of fruit pectin and follow the directions step-by-step. Here is a simple recipe for strawberry jam.

Strawberry Jam

5 Cups Strawberries, cleaned, tops removed)

1 Box Fruit Pectin

½ tsp. Butter

7 Cups Sugar

Sterilize jars and lids. Let the jars stand in hot water until time to fill. Drain before filling. Stem and crush strawberries and put in pan. Stir in pectin and butter. Bring mixture to a full rolling boil. Stir in sugar. Return to a full rolling boil. Boil exactly one minute, stirring constantly. Remove from heat.

Spoon into prepared jars to within ¼ inch from top. Cover with lid and screw bands on tightly. Lower jars into a canner, making sure water covers the jars. Cover and bring to a gentle boil for 10 minutes. Remove jars and place on a towel to cool.

Write a Poem about Homemaking

We have studied so much about homemaking this year and now we are talking about the art of writing. Let's write a poem about homemaking. Work on your poem and copy it in the box below.

Week Three Meet with Mom

Recite Proverbs 31.

Discuss *Hidden Art of Homemaking*

- Describe how Writing, Poetry, & Prose play a role in Homemaking.

Read Homemaking Poems Aloud.

Go Strawberry Picking

Make Strawberry Jam

Prayer Focus:

- Prayer Life

Week Three Home

Memorize Proverbs 31:10-31

Write Proverbs 31:10-31 in the version of your choice. I recommend NASB or NKJ or ESV. Then say the passage aloud.

Drama & Humor

Homemaking is preparing and maintaining a home for those you love. It is a ministry unto the Lord and a service for your family. What a great privilege it is to create a home!

Read *The Hidden Art of Homemaking,* Chapter #10

How does God display Drama?

_____

_____

_____

_____

_____

Where are some things in Scripture that are dramatic?

_____

_____

_____

_____

_____

_____

_____

Let's look at drama and humor. Jesus used humor such as a camel through the eye of a needle. God often had the prophets of the Old Testament do very dramatic things to illustrate His message to the people. Purity and wholesomeness is the key to drama and humor. Much worldly humor is indiscreet and unkind.

What can we do to bring drama into our homes?

_____

_____

_____

_____

We like to mimic sounds and do imitations. Some are quite funny. Your family might like to read poetry aloud, perform puppet shows, act out skits, and write plays. Improv games are a blast. We often play them at the children's birthday parties.

When my children were little, they loved acting out books they had read or Bible stories. Katie Beth once stuffed a big pillow in her shirt and stood on a chair. "I am Goliath," she said and continued to act out the story of David and Goliath with her little sister.

All families can enjoy drama by reading aloud. Don't stop reading aloud as children get older. Learn to be an expressive, pleasant reader that can keep an audience enthralled. Use different voices for different characters. Make noises. Reading aloud bonds a family together. It sharpens mental skills. It creates a hunger for good books. It helps children with their vocabulary and comprehension. It is fun!

Family Devotions

What a great way to add drama to family life. This special part of home life can have an impact even if only five minutes a day. Read the Bible aloud to children every day and then supplement with Bible storybooks and devotion books. We read the Bible aloud in the morning and Bible books in the evening. Have your children pray. Keep It Simple, simple! Read expressively and with a teachable heart yourself. Young children are not ready for intense Bible study; they need to become familiar with the entire Bible. There is always application but keep it simple. Again, be dramatic when you read the Bible and Bible stories aloud.

Create a Skit about Homemaking

Drama makes life more fun. Today, you will create a skit about homemaking. The skit can involve several people of just be a monologue.

Once the skit is finished, find some people to act it out with you. Videotape the skit and share it with others.

Title of my skit: _____

Who is in my skit: _____
_____
_____
_____
_____
_____

What is the basic plot of the skit: _____
_____
_____
_____
_____
_____
_____

How did the video turn out? _____
_____
_____
_____
_____

How to Take Great Photographs

It's time to talk about family photos. Often, Mom is the family photographer and storekeeper of memories.

Here are some tips to take good photographs.

Look your subject in the eye.

Use a plain background, if possible.

Use Gridlines to Balance Your Shot

Remember the "Rule of Thirds." In your mind, divide a photograph into third vertically and thirds horizontally. This will give you 9 little boxes with dividing lines. If you places the focal point in your image along one of these intersections, your photo will be balanced and aesthetically pleasing.

Focus on one subject. The subject should fill one-third of the photo and the other two-thirds should be negative space.

Try to get rid of clutter in the background. That is impossible in my house. The background has ruined so many great photos of mine!

Look for symmetry. Our eyes love balance and harmonious proportion in a photograph.

When possible, move closer and avoid using a zoom.

Use natural light when possible.

Look for small details.

Take candids.

Take some vertical photographs, instead of all horizontals.

Here are some tips to become a better photographer:

- Take your camera everywhere you go
- Take lots of pictures
- Visit parks and gardens. Plants and trees don't move so they are great to photograph
- Attend workshops
- Experiment with different angles; get down on your knees, stand on a chair, lay down on the ground
- Shoot during "Golden Hours" (early morning, late afternnon)

The Stay At Home Mom Book Review

By Donna Otto

What does Donna teach in Chapter 8 about a homemaker's wardrobe?

_____

_____

_____

_____

Why are mentors important for a homemaker (chapter 12)?

_____

_____

_____

_____

How can you keep order in your home (chapter 14)?

_____

_____

_____

_____

How can children help out at home (chapter 15)?

_____

_____

_____

_____

Talk about the financial implications of homemaking according to Donna (chapter 16 & 17).

_____

_____

_____

_____

Did you like this book? How will it help you as a homemaker?

_____

_____

_____

March: Making Memories

Memorize Proverbs 31

Jesus, Fill My Heart & Home Bible Study

Hidden Art of Homemaking

Photography & Scrapbooking

Birthdays

Make Proverbs 31 Book for Children

Optional: *HOME: God's Design* Book Review

(Meet with Mom weekly)

Week One Meet with Mom

Recite Proverbs 31.

Discuss *Hidden Art of Homemaking*

- Describe God and His Sense of Drama.
- Why is drama a good thing for a homemaker?

Discuss Photography

Perform Skit, or if you Videotaped it, Watch it

Scrapbooking

Prayer Focus:

- Thanking God for all His Blessing

Week One Home

Memorize Proverbs 31:10-31

Write Proverbs 31:10-31 in the version of your choice. I recommend NASB or NKJ or ESV. Then say the passage aloud.

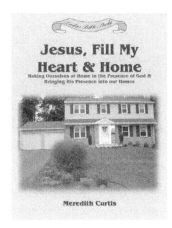

Jesus, Fill My Heart & Home Lesson 12

"Home: A Reflection of Heaven: A Welcome Center & A Celebration Center"

Read and Answer Questions

How to Store and Display Photos

Photographs are important to families, treasured for years to come.

Storing Digital Photos

Between phones, cameras, and sharing photos on Facebook and Instagram, our lives our filled with digital photos. I love digital photos and enjoy keeping up with friends online through their photos.

While some photos are fun, but not important, others are precious and should be saved for the future. Store digital photos in at least two places. I store mine on my desktop, One Drive, and an external hard drive. You can also store photos on SD cards, USB thumb drives, and i-Clouds.

Displaying Digital Photos

You can display digital photos on your online social sites, as well as special digital frames that are basically a mini-slide show scrolling through your favorite photos.

Storing Printed Photos

I have massive amounts of printed photographs since I have been taking pictures since I was eight years old. It has only been in the last few years that I have been able to limit what I print. In the old days, you took a roll of film and were stuck with the good and bad photos. I love digital!

I store most of my photos in albums with information on the back of every photograph (date, names in photo, location). This is because over the years we forgot who, what, and when the photo was taken.

I store extra photographs in special photo boxes and store them on a cool, dry shelf away from moisture and mold.

Photo Albums

Photo albums are such fun to pull out and look back at the "good old days." I am grateful that I invested time putting together these albums. My children love to pull them out and enjoy them.

Scrapbooks

Scrapbooking is fun! It is a way to save memories (ticket stubs, postcards) and photos together. I have an old scrapbook of my mother's and my grandmother's. What fun to see their creativity and get to know what they were like as young women. I scrapbooked as teen and later as a Mom.

Displaying Printed Photos

I print photos and put them in decorative frames on the walls and tabletops of my home. The piano is covered with photo frames that bring back memories.

Storing Old Photos

Old photos are delicate and should be handled with care. Often there are tiny rips and tears. For a fee, you can have them restored.

I suggested scanning older photos so that you can print from the jpeg if you want to make copies.

Displaying Old Photos

I love to frame old photos and hang them on the wall. It is just important to make sure the frame matches the photo in style.

How to Scrapbook

Scrapbooking has been around for a long time. Young girls filled scrapbooks with mementos and photographs. Scrapbooking is a way to express your style, personality, and passions.

Scrapbooking requires a few tools to get started. You will need:

- Scissors
- Photographs
- Scrapbooking Paper
- Decorative Scissors
- Acid-Free Paper to Frame Photos
- Stickers and Other Embellishments

You can make a single scrapbook page or work on an entire scrapbook. For each page, you will choose your photos and choose your theme to get started. If you have some photos of a beach trip, you may want to go with a nautical theme, using paper with ships on it and nautical stickers.

Here is a list of the photos I'm going to use:

_____   _____

_____   _____

_____   _____

My theme will be: _____

My main colors will be:

_____   _____

My accent colors will be:

_____   _____

I have chosen the following stickers and embellishments:

_____   _____

_____   _____

_____   _____

You will also need to plan the layout of your page or pages. For ideas on different layouts, you can check Pinterest or scrapbook sites online.

There is nothing wrong with a simple layout of four photos on a page:

Here are photos of my finished pages:

Week Two Meet with Mom

Recite Proverbs 31.

Discuss *Jesus, Fill My Heart & Home*

- Discuss ways to show hospitality.
- Discuss ways to make celebrations special.
- What is your favorite holiday?
- How do you celebrate that holiday?
- What are some ideas to celebrate holidays in your own home one day?

Scrapbook Together

Prayer Focus:

- Prayer Life

Week Two Home

Memorize Proverbs 31:10-31

Write Proverbs 31:10-31 in the version of your choice. I recommend NASB or NKJ or ESV. Then say the passage aloud.

How to Make Birthdays Special

Birthday were special events when I grew up. We got to pick out our favorite food for dinner, our chores were cancelled, and we had a lovely birthday party every year. I loved birthdays! Oh, and did I mention presents and cards from family and friends.

Here are some ways to make birthdays special for your family members.

- Tell a child the story of his/her birth
- Have a special plate that is only used on birthdays
- Honor the birthday person by having everyone tell him/her what they appreciate about him/her
- Pray over the birthday person
- Create a treasure hunt so the birthday person can follow clues to the birthday present
- A delicious breakfast in bed on a tray with a flower in vase and linen napkins
- Fill his or her bedroom with balloons while he/she sleeps
- Write a birthday message on the bathroom mirror
- Exempt birthday person from any chores or work around the house
- Make a birthday slideshow of the birthday person chronicling the last year
- Send care packages to a family member who is away from home with goodies, balloons, cards, and presents
- Do an annual birthday interview
- Display birthday cards
- Make the birthday person's favorite dinner
- Plan a special dessert or cake
- Plan a special birthday party

Birthday Party Ideas

Birthdays are a great reason to have a party. Birthday parties can be casual cake-and-ice cream events or they can be festive celebrations with themes, games, and special food.

Here are Some Ideas for Children's Parties.

- Little Princess Party with a huge cardboard castle, castle cake, children dress up as their favorite prince or princess, acting out fairy tales
- Wild, Wild West Party with children dressed as Cowboys or Indians, large tepee to listen to a picture book, games, sing cowboy songs, cowboy food
- Luau with hula dancing, limbo, Hawaiian food, dress Hawaiian, play games
- Circus with clowns, animal rides, carnival games, popcorn, cotton candy

- Truck Party with truck rides, truck cake, bowling to knock trucks over, color truck pictures, ride toy trucks

Here are Some Ideas for Teens & Adult Parties

- 50's Sock Hop with dressing 50's style, root beer floats, malted milkshakes, chili dogs, 50s music, hula hoops, and dancing
- Backyard BBQ with horseshoes, croquet, corn hole, grilling chicken, potato salad, baked beans
- Beach Party with volleyball, Frisbee, watermelon
- Old-Fashioned with charades, lip syncing, cake and ice cream

Make Birthdays Special Project

Whose birthday in your family is coming up next? It's time to plan a birthday party for them? Think about their interests, hobbies, and likes. What would be a special theme for his/her party? What games would he/she enjoy playing? How about food? Make a plan.

Birthday Theme: _____

Birthday Games: _____   _____

_____   _____   _____

_____   _____   _____

Food: _____   _____

_____   _____   _____

_____   _____   _____

Decorations: _____   _____

_____   _____   _____

_____   _____   _____

Proverbs 31 Books for Little Girls Project: "How to be a Good Wife and Mommy at Home"

You have been memorizing Proverbs 31 this year, reciting it, and copying the passage once a week. That is an important passage for us as women to know what is commendable to the Lord.

We will be doing a special project that will serve two purposes:

1. It will help you understand Proverbs 31 more
2. It will be a blessing to a little girl between 3 to 8 years old.

This week you will make a little booklet for young girls 3-8 years old about how to be a good wife and mother. Use pictures in your book. The pictures can be photographs, clip art, your own art, or printed pictures from the internet.

The idea for this booklet goes back to one that I made for little daughters. I cut out pictures from magazines and put them in a magnetic photo album (popular back in the day). Next to each illustration, I wrote down a verse on an index card, placing it next to the picture.

Years later, I gave the assignment to my daughers when they took this class in high school. Jenny Rose took computer paper folded in half and made a booklet. She illustrated each verse herself.

Julianna made hers on the computer and printed it out, placing it inside a 3-prong folder.

If you don't want to make a booklet, you can make a short video directed to children about how to be a good wife and mother.

You should have each verse from the passage on a separate page.

Think about what each verse means and how you would illustrate it.

When it says, "She speaks with kindness and laughs at the days to come," what comes to your mind? Do you see a young woman laughing? Do you see a mom doing something kind to her children? Do you see a mom with her children reaching out to the poor?

Think through each verse of the passage like this.

Photograph of My Booklet for Children: "How to be a Good Wife and Mommy at Home"

Week Three Meet with Mom

Recite Proverbs 31.

Share Proverbs 31 Book for Children

Share Birthday Party Ideas

Go Out to Eat at a Foreign Restaurant

Prayer Focus:

- Children in your life

Week Three Home

Memorize Proverbs 31:10-31

Write Proverbs 31:10-31 in the version of your choice. I recommend NASB or NKJ or ESV. Then say the passage aloud.

Creative Recreation, Traditions, Making Memories

𝕳𝖔𝖒𝖊𝖒𝖆𝖐𝖎𝖓𝖌 is preparing and maintaining a home for those you love. It is a ministry unto the Lord and a service for your family. What a great privilege it is to create a home!

Read *The Hidden Art of Homemaking,* Chapter #11

How does God encourage rest?

_____

_____

_____

_____

_____

What does He provide to get us rest and recreation?

_____

_____

_____

_____

_____

"*By* the seventh day God had finished the work he had been doing; so on the seventh day he rested from all his work. And God blessed the seventh day and made it holy, because on it he rested from all the work of creating that he had done*" (Genesis 2:2-3 NIV ©1979).

A principle here: Finish work and then celebrate with resting!

"So, because Jesus was doing these things on the Sabbath, the Jews persecuted him. Jesus said to them: 'My Father is always at his work to this very day, and I, too, am working'" (John 5:16-17 NIV ©1979).

"Therefore, since the promise of entering his rest still stands, let us be careful that none of you be found to have fallen short of it. For we also have had the gospel preached to us, just as they did; but the message they heard was of no value to them, because those who heard did not combine it with faith. Now we who have believed enter that rest, just as God has said.

"So I declared on oath in my anger, 'They shall never enter my rest." And yet his work has been finished since the creation of the world. For somewhere he has spoken about the seventh day in these words: 'and on the seventh day God rested from all his work.' And again in the passage above he says, 'They shall never enter my rest.'*

"It still remains that some will enter that rest, and those who formerly had the Gospel preached to them did not go in, because of their disobedience. Therefore God again set a certain day, calling it Today, when a long time later he spoke through David, as was said before:

"Today if you hear his voice, do not harden your hearts.'

"For if Joshua had given them rest, God would not have spoken later about another day. There remains therefore, a Sabbath rest for the people of God; for anyone who enters God's rest, also rests from his own work, just as God did from his. Let us, therefore, make every effort to enter that rest, so that no one will fall by following their example of disobedience" (Hebrews 4:1-11 NIV ©1979).

Three Kinds of Recreation:

1. Recreation to refresh your soul.
2. Recreation to refresh your body and mind.
3. Recreation that will create memories: celebrations and family traditions.

Spirit Refreshment only happens in the presence of God. Do not settle for anything but God's presence! Here are some ways to enjoy spiritual refreshment.

- Personal retreat or day away with Jesus
- Extra long Quiet Time or just worship time
- Retreat with lots of Bible teaching, worship and prayer
- Receiving personal prayer and ministry
- Reviewing all your favorite promises in the Bible and then thanking God for them
- Listening to praise music
- Listening to Bible tapes
- Fellowship

Our bodies and minds need rest and recreation too. It is nice to just relax and enjoy peace and quiet. Here are some ways to recreate.

- Hikes or nature walks
- Sports
- Aerobic activity to relieve stress
- Fine art museum, ballet, opera, or classical music concert
- Quiet walks on the beach
- Picnics in the park
- Sunbathing

Memory making is one of my favorite parts of being a homemaker. Memories are made in the little daily and weekly routines of life, as well as in the holidays and celebrations. Both are important. Sometimes it's great to make a memory by turning an ordinary day into something special—surprise the family!

Here are ways to make memories with your family:

- Treasure hunts and meal hunts
- Holiday traditions, meals and decorating
- Date nights
- Family nights
- Family vacations
- Romantic escapes
- Birthdays (child pick meal, BD tablecloth, BD person does no work, family day, family BD celebration, party with friends, laying on hands for prayer)
- Bedtime rituals
- Family devotions
- Family day trips (e.g. beach, zoo, Sea World, park, sightseeing)
- Projects around the house (e.g putting in a garden)
- Playing cards and games
- Celebrating milestones (e.g. Heart and key necklace, big girl panties, school book bag)
- Making and baking Christmas and other gifts together
- Reading aloud good books as adults and older children
- Playing sports (tennis, kickball, running, dancing)
- Music and singing nights
- Mom disciples teenage girls; Dad disciples teenage boys
- Daydreaming together as a family

Fantastic Family Night Fun

Are you ready to talk about family fun? We started family nights when our children were young. It felt a little silly to be honest because we were always together anyway. But, nonetheless we set aside one night a week to spend time together playing games, watching a movie, or doing something fun as a family. We made a nice dinner that night, too.

Now, we are so grateful for our family nights because some weeks it's the only time we see each other with our hectic schedules because the kids are older now working or going to college.

Food

A special night includes good food. Right now, Julianna makes us a special dinner every family night. She loves to cook and she tries out all kinds of new dishes on us. We are grateful!

Fun

There are so many possibilities. Board games are quite fun to play and many can be enjoyed by all ages. We like Hilarium®, Headbanz®, Guestures®, Outburst®, and Pictionary®.

Other games we like include the Dictionary Game, charades, and story games where one person starts a story and it is continued by the person next to them.

Outside fun includes croquet, corn hole, horse shoes, Frisbee, volleyball, and kickball.

In addition, we have done creative things like divide into groups, make up commercials, record them, and watch them together.

Sometimes we watch a movie.

Fantastic Family Night Fun Project

Now, it's your turn to plan a family night for your own family. Think about what each family member enjoys. What things do you and your family enjoy doing together? How about food?

Family Night Food: _____   _____

_____   _____   _____

_____   _____   _____

_____   _____   _____

Family Night Fun: _____   _____

_____   _____   _____

_____   _____   _____

Hostess a Family Fun Night

Once you have your family night plans, it's time to host the family night. Be sure to take photographs and paste a photo below.

How did the evening go? _____
_____
_____

What went well? _____
_____
_____
_____
_____

Did anything go wrong? _____
_____
_____
_____
_____

Cooking with an International Flair

One thing that is fun is to visit other countries, see the sights, and taste the food. Each country has its own flavor and charm. This month you will cook up dishes from another country.

Here are some international recipes from my geography cookbook, *Travel God's World Cookbook*: One from Germany, one from Nigeria, one from Taiwan, and one from South Africa.

Hot German Potato Salad

1 ½ Pounds Potatoes

3 Slices Bacon

1 Medium Onion, chopped

1 Tbsp. All-Purpose Flour

1 Tbsp. Sugar

1 tsp. Salt

¼ tsp. Celery Seed

Dash of Pepper

½ Cup Water

¼ Cup Vinegar

Put potatoes in salted water and bring to a boil. Reduce heat and cook until tender, 20-25 minutes. Cook bacon until crisp; drain. Cook onion in the bacon fat. Stir in flour, sugar, salt, celery seed, and pepper. Cook over low heat, stirring constantly until the mixture bubbles; remove from heat.

Stir in water and vinegar. Heat to boiling, stirring constantly. Let it boil 1 minute and keep stirring. Remove from heat.

Crumble bacon in the hot mixture. Slice warm potatoes and add to hot mixture. Cook, stirring gently, to coat potato slices. Cook until hot and bubbly. Serve warm

Taiwan Boba Tea, or Bubble Tea

Boba Tea originated in Taiwan in the 1980s and spread throughout Asia before coming to Europe and the United States.

You can find **Boba** at any Asian grocery store or online. What's really fun is that they come in a range of colors. Boba is tapioca pearls that are bigger than the little pearls we use for cooking and baking. Once you cook the boba, it's best to mix them with the sugar syrup to help produce the pearls you are not using right away.

2 Cups Water per ¼ Cup Dried Boba

¼ Cup Dried Boba Tapioca Pearls per serving

1-2 Tea Bags per serving, an flavor

½ Cup Water

½ Cup Sugar

Milk, Almond Milk, or Sweetened Condensed Milk

Prepare Cup of Strong Tea

Bring 1 cup of water per serving to boil and add teabags. Let tea steep for 15 minutes and remove teabag. Let tea cool before using in the Boba Tea.

Prepare Boba

Bring water to a rolling boil. Add boba and stir gently until they start to float on the top of the water. Lower heat and cook the boba for 12-15 minutes. Remove the pan from the heat and cover with a lid. Let boba sit covered for 12-15 minutes. Drain water from boba and add boba to a container. Pour syrup over the boba until they are submerged. Let boba sit at room temperature in syrup for 15 minutes or refrigerate. Boba is best used within a few hours of cooking, but you can store in the refrigerator for a few days.

Prepare Syrup

While the boba are cooking, make a simple syrup to sweeten the boba and preserve any extra boba. Bring water (1/2 cup per serving) to boil. Remove from heat and stir in the sugar until it dissolves.

Assemble the Boba Tea

Pour the tea into a small glass and add the boba. Add milk, almond milk, or sweetened condensed milk.

Nigerian Akara Balls

Akara balls are sold at Nigerian roadside stalls. When you buy them in Nigeria, you can choose from various spicy sauces to eat with the mild Akara Balls.

1 Can Black-Eyed Peas

Salt & Pepper to Taste

Oil for Deep-Frying

Drain can of black-eyed peas. Place beans with salt and pepper in blender and blend until beans are a paste. Add more water if needed. Fry spoonfuls of paste in a skillet. Turn until browned all over. Serve with mango chutney or another spicy sauce.

South African Chicken

6 Onions, sliced thin

6 Garlic Cloves, minced

¼ Cup Lemon Juice

Salt & Pepper to Taste

1 Whole Chicken, cut into serving pieces

1 Tbsp. Olive Oil

In large Ziplock® zipper-style bag, combine onions, garlic, lemon juice, salt, and pepper. Add chicken pieces and zip up bag. Roll the chicken around in the bag to coat. Refrigerate overnight to marinate. Remove chicken from marinade and pour marinade into the crockpot. Brown the chicken in a skillet and transfer to crockpot. Cover crockpot with lid and cook on low-setting for 4-6 hours, or until chicken is cooked through. Serve chicken with brown rice and spoon sauce over chicken.

HOME God's Design Book Review

By Miriam Huffman Rockness

Describe order, custom, and ceremony and their roles in creating a home for your family.

_____
_____
_____

How can a home be a shelter?

_____
_____
_____

Will you earn your bread, follow your trade, or build a cathedral? Why? _____
_____
_____
_____
_____

What is your personal style? How will you bring it into your home?

_____
_____
_____
_____

How can a homemaker open her home and show hospitality?

_____
_____
_____
_____

How does a homemaker instill a biblical worldview to her family?

_____
_____
_____
_____

April: Clothing & Relationships

Memorize Proverbs 31

Jesus, Fill My Heart & Home Bible Study

Hidden Art of Homemaking

Dream House Project

Cookies, Cake Decorating

Gardening

Optional: *A Woman and Her Home* Book Review

(Meet with Mom weekly)

Week One Meet with Mom

Recite Proverbs 31.

Discuss *Hidden Art of Homemaking*

- Describe God as a Provider of Rest & Recreation.
- What is your favorite way to relax?
- What is your favorite way to have fun?
- How does rest & recreation play a role in homemaking?

Share Family Night Experience

- What went well?
- What would you do differently?

Scrapbook

Prayer Focus:

- Your Future Home

Week One Home

Memorize Proverbs 31:10-31

Write Proverbs 31:10-31 in the version of your choice. I recommend NASB or NKJ or ESV. Then say the passage aloud.

Clothing

𝕳omemaking is preparing and maintaining a home for those you love. It is a ministry unto the Lord and a service for your family. What a great privilege it is to create a home!

Read *The Hidden Art of Homemaking*, Chapter #12

How does God cloth us? _____

_____

_____

_____

How does He clothe the lilies of the field and the animals? _____

_____

_____

_____

_____

Clothing

"But the LORD said to Samuel, 'Do not consider his appearance or his height, for I have rejected him. The LORD does not look at the things man looks at. Man looks at the outward appearance, but the LORD looks at the heart.'…So he sent and had him (David) brought in. He was ruddy, with a fine appearance and handsome features" (I Samuel 16:7 & 12 NIV ©1979)

God looks at the heart. He does not reject beauty, but does not choose someone because of it. People see the outside and form an opinion.

Read *The Hidden Art of Homemaking*, Chapter #12

"I also want women to dress modestly, with decency and propriety, not with braided hair or gold or pearls or expensive clothes, but with good deeds, appropriate for women who worship God" (I Timothy 2:9-10 NIV ©1979).

"Your beauty should not come from outward adornment, such as braided hair and the wearing of gold jewelry and fine clothes. Instead, it should be that of your inner self, the unfading beauty of a gentle and quiet spirit, which is of great worth in God's sight. For this is the way the women of the past who put their hope in God used to make themselves beautiful. They were submissive to their own husbands, like Sarah, who obeyed Abraham and called him her master. You are her daughters if you do what is right and do not give way to fear" (I Peter 3:3-6 NIV).

"When it snows, she has no fear for her household; for all of them are clothed in scarlet. She makes coverings for her bed; she is clothed in fine linen and purple" (Proverbs 31:21-22 NIV ©1979).

How you dress depends on the answer to this question: Who are you? You are a woman of God.

Our clothing should be dignified. After all we are royalty—our father is the King of Kings. Modesty should characterize the way we dress by covering up private parts and wearing loose clothing. Propriety is simple wearing the right outfit for the right occasion. We don't wear a gown to the beach and we don't wear a bathing suit to church. We should also have style, expressing our artistic side through our clothing.

"Then Jesus said to his disciples: 'Therefore I tell you, do not worry about your life, what you will eat; or about your body, what you will wear. Life is more than food, and the body more than clothes. Consider the ravens: They do not sow or reap, they have no storeroom or barn; yet God feeds them. And how much more valuable you are than birds! Who of you by worrying can add a single hour to his life? Since you cannot do this very little thing, why do you worry about the rest?

"Consider how the lilies grow. They do not labor or spin. Yet I tell you, not even Solomon in all his splendor was dressed like one of these. If that is how God clothes the grass of the field, which is here today, and tomorrow thrown in the fire, how much more will He clothe you, O you of little faith! And do not set your heart on what you will eat and drink; do not worry about it. For the pagan world runs after all such things, and your Father knows that you need them. But seek His kingdom, and these things will be added to you as well. Do not be afraid, little flock, for your Father has been pleased to give you the Kingdom" (Luke 12:22-32 NIV ©1979).

If God clothes the lilies so beautifully, will he not also cloth you beautifully? It is not godly to neglect your appearance and look frumpy and disheveled. Neither is it godly to dress seductively or immodestly. Try to look feminine, neat, clean and attractive.

Build My Wardrobe

We are going to talk about clothes and building a personal wardrobe that will withstand fashion fads.

Essential Wardrobe Basics

Here are some wardrobe basics. Buy quality so that they will last for decades, not years. These items are staples that stand the test of time and can be mixed and matched to make wonderful outfits and be prepared for unexpected occasions (like a funeral or job interview).

- Trench Coat
- Cashmere Wool Crew-Neck Sweater (for those who live in cold places)
- Denim Jacket
- Navy or Black Classic Blazer
- Comfortable Jeans in Good Repair
- Silk Blouse in White or Cream
- Cotton Button-Down Shirt in White or Cream
- Simple Black or Navy Dress
- Black or Navy Mid-Calf Skirt in Classic A-line Style
- Black or Navy Dress Pants
- White T-Shirt
- High Tank Tops for layering and wearing under low necklines

- White Long-Sleeved T-Shirt
- White or Cream Turtleneck
- Modest Bathing Suit that is Flattering
- Black or Brown Ankle Boots
- Strappy Sandal for Formal Events
- Black pumps
- Nice Flat Shoes
- Slip-On Sneakers
- Comfortable Flip-Flops (like Crocs®)

You will hold on to these pieces for years to come and they will come in handy when you least expect it.

Which of the wardrobe essential basics do you already have?

_____   _____   _____

_____   _____   _____

_____   _____   _____

_____   _____   _____

_____   _____   _____

Which pieces in the wardrobe essential basics do you want to acquire?

_____   _____   _____

_____   _____   _____

_____   _____   _____

You can ask for these essentials as gifts and save up money to purchase them yourselves. Acquire them slowly over time and be willing to spend money for quality clothing and shoes that will last for decades, not years. You get what you pay for. Speaking of shopping.

How to Shop for Clothes

Most ladies love to shop for clothes and shoes. Here are some tips to help you find great clothes for yourself and your family.

- Make a List. Decide beforehand what you are shopping for. Think of key pieces you need and focus on finding those items

- Check the Care Label. Is it Dry Clean Only? Does Anyone in your Family go to a Dry Cleaner. If no, Put it Back
- Make a Budget. Stick to the Budget. Bring Cash if Possible so you are not Tempted to Charge
- Be willing to Pay More for Quality, but Watch Out for High Prices
- Wear Comfortable Clothing that is Easy to get On and Off. Wear Slip-On Shoes that Come Off Easily
- Try On Everything that Catches your Eye—things look so different on you than the hanger
- Don't Buy Something Without Trying it on
- Take the Size you think you are to the Dressing Room, along with One Size Smaller and One Size Bigger
- Think about the Rest of the Clothing at Home. Does this Piece Fit in with Other Things you Own? Can it be Mixed & Matched to Make Several Different Outfits?
- Touch the Fabric—you can tell a lot about the garment's quality from touching the fabric
- Inspect Clothing for Fabric Tears, Seam Rips, Puckering Sleeves, Uneven Hems, Missing Buttons, or Gap that open when you sit down. Does the zipper work?
- Ask yourself: "Does it Feel Like Me?" and "Am I Comfortable in this?"

Here are Some Don'ts

- Don't Go Shopping when you have your period or are bloated
- Don't Go Clothes Shopping When you are Sick or Look Bad
- Don't Go Shopping when you Feel Emotional
- Don't Buy Something Just because It's on Sale
- Don't Purchase Clothing that is too High-Maintenance

Clothing a Houseful

Clothing an entire household can be a challenge. You start out with marriage where you move from single (lots of great clothes) to an immediate smaller clothing budget. When the first baby comes along, you are lavished with sparkling new outfits that are quickly stained. As more babies come along, there are less and less clothes presented. Soon you are handing down outfits from one child to the next one.

Some of my children were easy on clothes and other destroyed them. Some outfits lasted longer than I would have dreamed. I still see some children at church wearing clothing that has been around since the 1980s. Wow! That's long-lasting clothing.

Let's talk about children's clothing. Since I only wash once a week, I suggest enough clothing for a whole week.

Here are some wardrobe basics for little boys:

- 7-8 pairs underwear
- 2 pairs of pajamas (can be worn several nights without washing)
- 6-7 casual shirts
- 1 dress shirt
- 2 pairs jeans
- 1 pair dress pants
- 4 pairs shorts
- 7-8 pairs socks
- 1 pair sneakers
- 1 pair dress shoes

Here are some wardrobe basics for little girls:

- 7-8 pairs panties
- 2 nightgowns (can be worn several nights without washing)
- 2 play dresses
- 1 church dress
- 1 pair jeans
- 4 pairs shorts
- 7-8 pairs socks
- 1 pair sneakers
- 1 pair sandals
- 1 pair church shoes

How to Handle Hand-Me-Downs

We have handed down all our children's clothes to the younger children. Here is how we do it.

When one of the children outgrows a group of clothing, the clothing is all washed, folded, and put away in a large storage tote. Then the storage tote is labeled with the size of the clothing inside.

Since I live in Florida, I cannot store these children in an attic or garage because they need to be stored in air-conditioning to protect them from insects, humidity, and mold. I store the totes in the closet under the stairs.

When it's time to get the clothes out for the younger children, the clothing is washed again, folded, and put away.

Week Two Meet with Mom

Recite Proverbs 31.

Discuss *Hidden Art of Homemaking*

- Describe God as a Provider of Coverings & Clothing.
- How can our clothing honor Christ?
- How can our clothing reflect our personality?

Put Together Outfits with the Wardrobe Essentials

Put Together Outfits by Adding Fashion Fads to Wardrobe Essentials

Prayer Focus:

- Outward Appearance/Inner Heart

Week Two Home

Memorize Proverbs 31:10-31

Write Proverbs 31:10-31 in the version of your choice. I recommend NASB or NKJ or ESV. Then say the passage aloud.

Accessorize

One of the fun thing about clothing is accessorizing. Accessories turn pants and a shirt into an outfit.

Accessories include belts, scarves, jewelry, and hats.

Make a list of your favorite accessories:

_____   _____   _____

_____   _____   _____

_____   _____   _____

_____   _____   _____

Experiment with accessories and clothing to create several different looking outfits. Take photos of your new outfits and paste one here.

Care of Clothing, Shoes, Accessories

We have already talk about laundry and check the labels on clothing before you wash it. Now, let's talk about other things we can do to take good care of our clothing, shoes, and accessories.

Keep clothing clean; wash it after you wear it. Don't pile dirty clothing on top of clean clothing.

Once clothing is clean, put it away immediately. Don't leave laundry sitting unfolded.

Make sure that you store clothing so that it hangs properly in the closet without being squished or wrinkled. Protect clothing from sticky hands, spills, water, and other things that can damage it. Children shouldn't play in closets or pull on the hems of clothing.

Clothing stored in drawers should be stored in neat piles after folding carefully. You may consider rolling up knit shirts, tanks, and skirts before putting them in drawers.

Don't store real gold or silver jewelry in the same container as imitation jewelry. Make sure that jewelry is not able to get tangled up with other pieces. I like to use little boxes in my jewelry drawer for storage. I store like things together.

Scarves can be folded or hung. I drape my long scarves over a hanger. Hangers work to hold ties as well.

Old-fashioned hat boxes are a great place to store hats. They protect them from being smooshed.

Don't store shoes in a big pile. Store them on shoe shelves or shoe racks. If you walk in mud, wipe shoes or boots off immediately.

Be careful when ironing that the iron is not too hot.

Button buttons before hanging clothing up, especially the top button. Zip zippers before washing, but also before storing. An open zipper can damage other clothing.

Week Three Meet with Mom

Recite Proverbs 31.

Go Clothes Shopping, Try on Outfits

Gather a Bunch of Hats, Belts, Scarves, Jewelry, and other Accessories. Give the same outfit different looks using different accessories.

Prayer Focus:

- Health of people in your life.

Week Three Home

Memorize Proverbs 31:10-31

Write Proverbs 31:10-31 in the version of your choice. I recommend NASB or NKJ or ESV. Then say the passage aloud.

Integration/Mixing It Up

Homemaking is preparing and maintaining a home for those you love. It is a ministry unto the Lord and a service for your family. What a great privilege it is to create a home!

Read *The Hidden Art of Homemaking,* Chapter #13

How does God integrate? _____
_____
_____
_____
_____

What blessing comes to us from being with people of different ages, backgrounds, and races? _____
_____
_____
_____
_____

We like to separate people according to age, marital status, intelligence level, and financial status. But, is that biblical?

"From one man He made every nation of men, that they should inhabit the whole earth; and he determined the times set for them and the exact places where they should live. God did this so that men would seek Him and perhaps reach out for Him and find Him, though He is not far from each one of us" (Acts 17:26-27 NIV ©1979).

What does this verse teach about the time and place we live?

_____
_____
_____
_____

"After this I looked and there before me was a great multitude that no one could count, from every nation, tribe, people and language, standing before the throne and in front of the Lamb. They were wearing white robes and were holding palm branches in their hands" (Revelation 7:9-10 NIV ©1979).

What variety does this show about God's family?

_____
_____
_____
_____

"Then little children were brought to Jesus for Him to place His hands on them and pray for them. But the disciples rebuked those who brought them. Jesus said, "Let the little children come to me, and do not hinder them, for the kingdom of heaven belongs to such as these." When He had placed his hands on them, he went on from there" (Matthew 19:13-15 NIV ©1979).

How does God view and value children?

_____
_____
_____
_____

"Do not rebuke an older man harshly, but exhort him as if he were your father. Treat younger men as brothers, older women as mothers, and younger women as sisters with absolute purity" (I Timothy 5:1-2 NIV ©1979).

Timothy was a young, single pastor. What advice does Paul give him and why?

_____
_____
_____
_____
_____

What principle can we glean from these verses?

_____
_____
_____
_____
_____

"Love must be sincere. Hate what is evil; cling to what is good. Be devoted to one another in brotherly love. Honor one another above yourselves. Never be lacking in zeal but keep your spiritual fervor serving the Lord. Be joyful in hope, patient in affliction, faithful in prayer. Share with God's people who are in need; practice hospitality. Bless those who persecute you; bless and do not curse. Rejoice with those who rejoice; mourn with those who mourn. Live in harmony with one another. Do not be proud but be willing to associate with people of a low position. Do not be conceited" (Romans12:9-16 NIV ©1979).

This passage gives us a picture of how the church should interact with one another. Share some commands and principles in this passage?

_____
_____
_____
_____
_____

Who is this passage addressed to: leaders? Children? Women? Young marrieds? Singles?

_____

_____

"If you have any encouragement from being united with Christ, if any comfort from his love, if any fellowship with the Spirit, if any tenderness and compassion, then make my joy complete by being like-minded, having the same love, being one in spirit and purpose. Do nothing out of selfish ambition or vain conceit, but in humility, consider others better than yourselves. Each of you should look not only to your own interests, but also to the interests of others.

"Your attitude should be the same as that of Christ Jesus: Who, being in very nature God, did not consider equality with God something to be grasped but made himself nothing, taking the nature of a servant, being made in human likeness. And being found in appearance as a man, he humbled himself and became obedient to death, even death on a cross! Therefore, God exalted him to the highest place and gave him the name that is above every name, that at the name of Jesus every knee should bow and every tongue confess that Jesus Christ is Lord to the glory of God the Father" (Philippians 2:1-11 NIV ©1979).

What keys to building relationships with other people are in this passage?

_____

_____

_____

_____

_____

_____

_____

What principles in this passage can help us overcome barriers such as age, race, language, interests, or theology?

_____

_____

_____

_____

_____

The key to building a friendship is not compatibility or common interests or similar life situations. The key is kindness, humility and JESUS!

Human relationships are the canvas. We "paint" with conversation, communication, and community living.

Spend Time with Someone from Another Generation

We lived in an age-segregated society. Even at church, you see the children go off in one direction, teens in another, singles in another, and retired folks in another. Did God create us to segregate by age? Is it helpful or harmful?

If we traveled back in time to the 1800s, we would find that age was not a really big deal. Students at schools were anywhere in age from 3 to 25.

Unbelievers who embraced the brand-new belief in psychology were the ones to address age and label "normal behavior" for certain ages. As the 20th century progressed, age-segregated institutions were build: elementary schools, high schools, nursing homes, and day care centers. No longer was life filled with all age groups.

But we don't have to live that way. We can enjoy people of all ages, building friendships and spending time together. God places people in families (various ages) and extended families (various ages). He calls his church a family made up of various nationalities, ages, and gifts.

What happens to people who are segregated by age?

- They think only in terms of their own season and its specific needs, tasks, and benefits (self-centered)
- Cannot understand what older or younger people are going through because it is so rare they hear about it (lack of compassion)
- They miss out on all the "stories" of the past from real people who did exciting things (lack of education)
- They miss out on life lessons their parents and grandparents learned (lack of mentoring)
- They cannot learn from older people in natural settings about life, work, family, and values (lack of mentoring)
- They are unable to pass on their own life lessons to younger people in a natural way (lack of mentoring others)

Age segregation fosters stereotyping of other age groups, mistrust between age groups, and misunderstanding.

Age has become an artificial barrier, separating people from people in other generations.

Name the people you spend time with on a regular basis who are from another generation:

_____   _____   _____

_____   _____   _____

_____   _____   _____

Now, choose someone you know from another generation that you don't see often, but you would like to spend time with: _____

Set up a plan with that person to spend time together. What will you do together? _____
_____
_____
_____
_____

After you spend time together, you will write a blog post on your experience. Here are some things to think about when you write your blog post.

My Audience: _____

Main Idea I want to Communicate: _____
_____
_____
_____
_____

How I will Express my Main Idea: _____
_____
_____
_____
_____

A blog post should be short. Make your post between 500 and 600 words.

My daughter Jenny Rose wrote about her experience years ago spending time with another generation. I found it years later and made it into a blog post.

A Generational Ornament

Here is the blog post with Jenny Rose's observations about spending time with another generation.

A Generational Ornament
By Jenny Rose Curtis (Age 14)

Making Christmas Ornaments with Grandma
Generational Ornament
PowerlineProd.com

I found this sweet essay my daughter Jenny Rose wrote after my mother passed away. In it is a message that you will appreciate and enjoy.

How wonderful person that the human race is made up of people of all ages and in different stages of life. It's a beautiful thing to be a part of time spent with people of different generations. Memories and growth come from a parent with their baby, a child with their elderly neighbor, or even a teenager with a mom that has six children! What every relationship has in common is learning from each other's lives and experiencing the amazing differences and similarities. The beauty comes from bridges that are gapped between the ages and love flowing from acceptance and admiration. The time spent together doesn't have to have a limit. It could be a minute, an hour, or a whole day. In my case, it was a week.

My family drove down to my grandparent's house in Pembroke Pines when I was ten years old. It was decided that I would spend a week with them until they came back up to Lake Mary for Katie Beth's graduation. I was excited. A whole week on my own with my grandparents! While I missed my family a lot, I had a good time there. I read, ate, played cards and, of course, got on the computer. But what stood out to me the most was making ornaments with Baba. She was so good at it, better than I ever could hope to be. She so gracefully and skillfully poured the paint into the glass ball ornament and twisted and turned it when the time came. I tried my best, I really did, but for some reason they just never turned out quite like hers. I don't think I would have even finished them if she hadn't encouraged me and helped me!

What Baba did for me was more than just teach how to make paint-filled ornaments, although that is a nice skill to have. She showed me love by spending time with me and enjoying it. She gave me the gift of a grandmother being proud of her grandchild, something no one else can quite give like her. Even when I ruined my ornaments, she would just encourage me and tell me to keep at it and not give up on what I've put my hands to. She taught me to have patience with myself and the things I do. No matter what I put my hands to, I must have patience and perseverance to complete them well. A gentle word of praise kept me going until we had finished them all.

As much as all of those things helped me grow, what I treasure the most was that it benefitted her too. Nothing made me happier than seeing some of the ornaments we made together put in a place of honor on a little table or the big piano. It meant something to me to know that it meant something to her. Those little worthless balls of glass and paint were brought to life when we made them together because even if they weren't perfect, they were full of love and memories.

A sharp twinge of remorse and hurt shot through me when I watched one break two years ago. However, I realized then that it wasn't the ornaments themselves that were special, but rather what they represented, the special time that Baba and I spent together. And even though she's in Heaven and I'm still here, I know that she still loves me and is proud of me. So as great as it is to spend time with another generation, it's even better when it's with a person that you love and loves you back.

Caring for the Elderly Project

We will discuss care of elderly friends today.

Families are responsible to care for the needy within its own family first. When our parents and grandparents age, they need help with normal everyday activities that they used to do themselves. It is our privilege to serve them. In this way, we fulfill the law of Christ. It is not the government's responsibility to care for our family members, it is ours.

Changes in the Elderly

As you grow older things change because the body is decaying. This happens because of what Adam and Eve did by sinning against God, bringing death into the world. Your body will decay too—yuck! But, we have heavenly bodies to look forward to that will never grow old! Isn't that great?

There are changes in the sensory system (sight, hearing, taste, touch, smell) and how they function in the elderly. Basically, the sensory receptors are less efficient and need higher levels of stimulation (louder voices, stronger light, more seasoning in food). The biggest problem with hearing and vision loss is that it can lead to a sense of isolation for our older friends.

Here are some of the visual changes that happen to the elderly.

- Acuity (sharpness)
- Farsightedness (need reading glasses)
- Color perception (greens, blues, and purples blur together)
- Decreased sensitivity to light (takes longer to adjust to a dark room or sudden bright light)
- Increased sensitivity to glare (shiny surfaces often produce glare for them)
- Possible Cataracts (lens gets cloudy and distorts vision—surgery will fix this!)
- Possible Glaucoma (high pressure on eye and optic nerve can lead to blindness—important for visits to eye doctor)
- Possible Macular Degeneration (cells in macula break down—lose central, but not peripheral vision)

Here are some ways to help older people with vision challenges.

- Use white paper with a dull finish and large black lettering
- Give them large print books
- Give them books on tape to listen to
- Use coding schemes (e.g. big colored dots at different places on the oven dial)
- Simplify visual field (remove clutter)
- Don't move anything in their world without telling them you have moved it
- Give pre-warnings when approaching
- Use touch to enhance communication
- When entering a new environment, explain people present and where they are located

- When walking, allow them to hold on to your arm just above the elbow and walk a half step ahead

Here are some of the changes the elderly experience in hearing.

- Sounds are more muffled
- High pitch sounds are distorted (harder to hear young children)
- Cannot make out words (words sound the same)

Here are some clues that an older person has difficulty hearing

- Accuses you of mumbling
- Talks very loudly or very softly
- Positions their head to hear better
- Asks speaker to repeat what has just been said
- Fails to respond
- Withdraws from social interaction
- Is distracted easily
- Is suspicious of others and what they are saying.

Here are some things that might help.

- Hearing aids
- Speak clearly in a moderate voice
- Get his/her attention before speaking
- Face person directly and at same level
- Use facial expressions, gestures, and objects to help you communicate
- Speak slowly and distinctly, but do not exaggerate with your lips
- Remove objects from your mouth when speaking (gum, food)
- Use longer pauses between sentences
- Decrease background noises
- Speak into their "good ear"
- Keep your voice at the same volume throughout a sentence
- My dad loved using "TV Ears" to watch television.

Elderly people also lose their sense of taste, smell, and touch. Realize that food won't taste or smell as good to them and it's not your cooking! Do everything you can to make food attractive and interesting. Find things that still taste and smell good; make them often.

Check up on them often, making sure they are not hurt…because they might cut or burn themselves and not realize it because of sensory loss.

Probably the hardest thing for older people to deal with is their loss of strength agility, and memory. Their minds and bodies simply won't do what they used to do. It is humiliating and frustrating. They can be grumpy, but it does not have anything to do with you.

Helping Aging Parents & Relatives

The best way to help aging parents, grandparents, or other aging relatives is to talk to them about aging before it happens. What are their wishes? Make plans, but realize that things change. We always thought Daddy would go first and Mom would come live with me because Daddy did NOT want to move back to Sanford. But Mom died first and Daddy moved back to Sanford. He did not want to live with us in our home, but, instead, chose an assisted living facility two minutes away. I was able to see him every day. Things turned out differently than we had planned.

One of the things that I regret was not staying in touch with my parents as much as I should have. I was busy raising five children, homeschooling, and being a pastor's wife. I would go months without talking to them. Before they died, I got into a habit of calling once a week. They looked forward to these calls and it was not hard to make it a habit.

Here are some things you can do to honor and be a blessing to your parents (and other aging relatives).

- Call once a week at the same time (older people love routine and this will be a highlight of their life!)
- Visit at least once or twice a year
- Write letters, notes, emails
- Foster a strong relationship between your parents and your children
- Focus on the good and forget the bad from the past—be thankful for your parents
- Remember them on birthdays, Mother's Day, Father's Day, St. Valentine's Day, Christmas
- Resolve any bitterness, ongoing quarrels, or battle of words

My parents needed my help just when my life was at its craziest and busiest. I had toddlers and teenagers, was homeschooling, and having medical problems of my own. It was hard to juggle everything, be faithful to my responsibilities at home, and honor my parents. I was honest with them when I couldn't do something and did my best to support them. I always tried to honor their decisions, even if I had a better plan. It was a privilege to care for them and I don't regret a single thing I did to help them at the end of their lives.

What is Caregiving?

When older people need care, you move into a role of caregiver. The care needed can be simple or very complicated depending on health and mental faculties.

Here are some of the tasks a caregiver might do:

- Making phone calls
- Shopping
- Managing financial and legal affairs
- Supervising medications
- Arranging for medical care
- Doctor visits
- Pharmacy visits
- Social outings
- Pushing/transporting wheelchairs/walkers/oxygen
- Listening, talking, providing emotional support
- Lifting/bathing/dressing/feeding
- Managing incontinence
- Supervision 24/7
- Supervise people who give direct care
- Traveling to and from his/her home
- Maintaining your home and his/her home

When Caregiving is Stressful

Caregiving is stressful and causes some or all of the following:

- Emotional exhaustion and sadness
- Physical exhaustion
- Depression
- Marital problems
- Family problems
- Conflict between your life roles: spouse, parent, employee, caregiver
- Neglect of the older person

Here are some things to keep you sane.

- Pray and have people cover you in prayer
- Ask for and accept help from family and friends (be specific!)
- Set a realistic schedule and stick to it
- Take care of yourself physically (diet, exercise, sleep, down time)

Caregiving from a Distance

This is so hard. I logged so many miles on my van driving back and forth from Lake Mary to Pembroke Pines. Then, when I moved Daddy to Sanford, my sister, Julie, was the long-distance caregiver. She handled all of Daddy's finances and I handled all of his physical and medical care. She flew down often and kept in touch with both Daddy and me.

Here are some tips for caregiving at a distance:

- Establish a network of people in your parent's world who will take care of them and keep in touch with you (relatives, church family, friends, neighbors, professionals)
- Lavish the local caregiver(s) with praise and thanks. You cannot appreciate them enough because the day-to-day is VERY hard! Bring gifts for them when you come to town
- Keep in touch with your parent as often as possible
- Be prepared to hop on a plane for emergencies (have your own world set up to do this)

The elderly often love visits from children and teenagers. If you can visit elderly relatives, do so. It is so exciting to hear their stories from the "old days." Though they often don't remember what happened last week, they can remember old stories in vivid detail.

Offer to take care of little things for older people including lawn care, shopping, reaching things on high shelves, minor repairs around the house, and getting the mail.

You can be a blessing!

Spend Time with an Elderly Person

This week, you will spend some time with an older person and do something to serve them. You might dust and vacuum their living room, mow their lawn, walk their dog, wash their car, or read aloud to them.

Choose an Elderly Person to Spend Time with: _____

What did you do to serve? _____
_____
_____
_____
_____

How was the experience? _____
_____
_____
_____
_____
_____

A Woman and Her Home Book Review

By Ella May Miller

Why is marriage and mothering so important?

_____

_____

_____

_____

What does Ella May say about materialism?

_____

_____

_____

_____

How can fear impede homemaking?

_____

_____

_____

Rediscovering the Joy of Serving God in the Place Where Life Really Matters

Ella May Miller

How does busyness impede homemaking?

_____

_____

_____

How can a homemaker limit activities to be more effective?

_____

_____

_____

Talk about trouble. How does a homemaker deal with trouble and loneliness?

_____

_____

_____

_____

hat role does love and forgiveness play in homemaking?

_____

_____

_____

_____

May: A Heart of Welcome

Memorize Proverbs 31

Hidden Art of Homemaking

Write Essay: "Homemaking, a Noble Career"

Hostess a Lady's Mother's Day Tea

Homemaking Panal

(Meet with Mom weekly)

Week One Meet with Mom

Recite Proverbs 31.

Discuss *Hidden Art of Homemaking*

- Why do you think God designed His family to be inter-generational?
- What do you learn from spending time with people of different ages?

Read Blog Post Aloud

Role Play Caring for Elderly or Sick

Prayer Focus:

- Elderly Friends

Week One Home

Memorize Proverbs 31:10-31

Write Proverbs 31:10-31 in the version of your choice. I recommend NASB or NKJ or ESV. Then say the passage aloud.

My Essay Outline: Homemaking, a Noble Career

Today you will write an essay on homemaking. You have studied this topic all year. I want you to write an essay to a brand-new wife who is thinking about staying home. Decide what your message to her will be.

Title: _____

Thesis Statement: _____
_____
_____
_____
_____

Introduction: _____
_____
_____
_____
_____
_____
_____

Main Point 1: _____
_____
_____
_____
_____

   Illustrations: _____
_____
_____
_____

   Subpoints: _____
_____
_____
_____
_____

Main Point 2: _____

_____

_____

_____

_____

    Illustrations: _____

_____

_____

_____

    Subpoints: _____

_____

_____

_____

Main Point 3: _____

_____

_____

_____

_____

    Illustrations: _____

_____

_____

_____

    Subpoints: _____

_____

_____

_____

_____

Plan & Hostess a Lady's Mother's Day Tea

This will be a fun project. You will plan and hostess a lady's Mother's Day Tea. You will need to plan a menu, guest list, activities, a devotional, and decorations.

Theme: _____

Menu: _____   _____

_____   _____   _____

_____   _____   _____

_____   _____   _____

_____   _____   _____

Decorations: _____   _____

_____   _____   _____

_____   _____   _____

_____   _____   _____

_____   _____   _____

Activities: _____   _____

_____   _____   _____

_____   _____   _____

_____   _____   _____

_____   _____   _____

Week Two Meet with Mom

Recite Proverbs 31.

Discuss Plans for Ladies' Mother's Day Tea

Read Essay Aloud

Homemaker Panel

Prayer Focus:

- Mothers

Homemaker Panel

We are commanded in Scripture to learn from older women and older women are commanded to teach younger women.

Today you will learn from several older women at one times. Ask 4-8 homemakers to join you today, to serve on a panel.

You and your friends will ask questions and listen to what they have to say. The topic is homemaking.

Come prepared with questions to ask about homemaking, hospitality, relationships, housekeeping, creativity in the home, creating a nurturing environment, and staying close to Jesus.

Write down a few questions here:

_____
_____
_____
_____
_____
_____
_____
_____
_____
_____
_____

Week Two Home

Memorize Proverbs 31:10-31

Write Proverbs 31:10-31 in the version of your choice. I recommend NASB or NKJ or ESV. Then say the passage aloud.

Environment

Homemaking is preparing and maintaining a home for those you love. It is a ministry unto the Lord and a service for your family. What a great privilege it is to create a home!

Read *The Hidden Art of Homemaking,* Chapter #14

What is it like to be in God's Presence?

____

____

____

____

What kind of environment does He create?

____

____

____

____

____

Homemaking involves creating an environment by who we are, not just what we do or say. If we want to bring the Presence of God into our homes, we must be filled with His Presence.

What is environment?

____

____

____

____

____

How do we affect the environment of our home as homemakers?

____

____

____

____

____

What things can we do or say that will make the environment more positive?

_____
_____
_____
_____

What things can we do or say that will make the environment more negative?

_____
_____
_____
_____

You are an artist, made in the image of the Perfect Artist. You are His artwork. Your home is His artwork. Partner with Him to bring life and beauty into your home, to make your home a reflection of Heaven.

Remember that you will set the atmosphere of your home. Be what God created you to be: a worshipper of Jesus, a follower of Jesus, a disciple of Jesus. Abide in Christ and your will bear good fruit, but apart from Him you can do nothing.

Clothe yourself with love and let His love fill you to overflowing so that your home will be a place of joy!

People Who Create a Positive Environment

Do you know people who create a positive environment?

There are people I know who walk into a room and instantly the room is cheery and sunny. They focus on other people, not themselves. Everyone feels valuable when they are around.

I want you to think of people who create a positive environment. What kind of environment to do they create?

Now, analyze them. What things do they do to create that positive atmosphere?

Put your findings in the chart on the next page.

Positive Environment Chart

Person	Environment they Create	How They Create It

Questions & Answers about Homemaking

What are different seasons in homemaking?

_____
_____
_____
_____
_____
_____

Why is homemaking valuable to the family, church and nation?

_____
_____
_____
_____
_____
_____

Why do women feel pressured to work outside the home?

_____
_____
_____
_____
_____
_____

Why do men need a homemaker in their lives?

_____
_____
_____
_____
_____
_____

Week Three Meet with Mom

Recite Proverbs 31.

Discuss *Hidden Art of Homemaking*

- How does the environment affect us?

Fashion Show with Dress You Made

Talk about How to Create a Positive Environment

Prayer Focus:

- Elderly Friends

Week One Home

Memorize Proverbs 31:10-31

Write Proverbs 31:10-31 in the version of your choice. I recommend NASB or NKJ or ESV. Then say the passage aloud.

Resources

Homemaking Skills Chart

Bible Study Worksheets

Orthodox Christianity

God's Girls Homemaking Skills Checklist

It's time to think about the practical skills needed to be a good wife and mother. Here is a check list of things that homemakers are often called on to do. Browse through this skill list and then go back and evaluate yourself on each skill. Is it something you do regularly, something you can do, but don't do often, or something you still need to learn to do? Talk to Mom and see if she will help you grow in these skill areas.

Homemaking Skill	My Ability	Part of my Daily Life?
Make Bed, Keep Room Tidy		
Cook Variety of Food/Meals		
Cook Gourmet Foods		
Bake Bread, Cookies, Pies, & Cakes		
Shop Efficiently, Saving Money, Getting Good Buys		
Plan Monthly Menu & Weekly Shopping List		
Set Formal Table		
Sort, Fold, & Put Away Laundry		
Ironing		
Housekeeping, Cleaning		
Control Clutter, Keep House Tidy		
Interior Decorating		
Flower Arranging		
Pet & Livestock Care		
Gardening		
Canning		

Homemaking Skill	My Ability	Part of my Daily Life?
Organize Drawers, Files, Cupboards, & Closets		
Organize Papers & Business Documents		
Tithe & Pay Bills		
Make Family Budget		
Live On Budget for a Long Time		
Plan & Save Money for Needed & Desired Items		
Plan & Budget for Family Trips & Vacations		
Make Goals & Attain Them		
Delegate Authority & Jobs with Confidence		
Problem Solve		
Communicate Kindly, Clearly, & Truthfully		
Listening & Asking Questions Skills		
Resolve Conflict Lovingly		
Forgive		
Respond in Love when People are Mean, Angry, or Rude to you		
Be a Peacemaker, Help Others Walk through Conflict		

Homemaking Skill	My Ability	Part of my Daily Life?
Healthy Habits during Pregnancy		
Baby Care		
Teach Bible to Young Children		
Lead Little Ones to Christ		
Understand Children's Developmental Stages & How to Train Children at Each Stage		
Read Aloud Expressively		
Homeschool and Tutor		
Respond Calmly and with Wisdom in Medical Emergencies		
Administer First Aid		
Care for the Sick		
Care for the Elderly		
Use Herbs & Homemade Remedies for Sickness & Accidents		
Plan a Wedding		
Plan a Funeral		
Understand & Experience Menopause Gracefully		

Homemaking Skill	My Ability	Part of my Daily Life?
Make Birthdays & Holidays Special		
Plan Traditions & Celebrations to Create Happy Memories		
Decorate for Parties, Birthdays, & Special Events		
Send Birthday Cards		
Choose, Wrap, & Give Gifts that will Bless Others		
Hostess Parties, Teas, Showers, BBQs, Children's Parties & Special Events		
Preserve Family Memories		
Photography		
Scrapbooking		
Videotaping & Family Movies		
Framing & Hanging Pictures		
Stock a Family Library with Good Books & Classic Literature		
Stock a Family Music Collection		

Homemaking Skill	My Ability	Part of my Daily Life?
Simple Sewing		
Sew Own Clothing		
Embroidery		
Cross-Stitch		
Knit		
Crochet		
Rug Hook, Rug Braid		
Other Needlecraft		
Crafts of all Kinds		
Paint		
Sing		
Play Instruments		
Express Self through Writing		
Tell Jokes, Anecdotes & Stories		
Enjoy Life to the Fullest!		

Bible Study Worksheet

Book and Chapter_____Date_____

Key verse to memorize_____
_____
_____
_____

Observations (interesting things you notice about people, place, time, atmosphere, situation, etc.):_____
_____
_____
_____
_____
_____
_____

Choose a title for each paragraph:

_____
_____
_____
_____
_____
_____
_____

How are the paragraphs related to each other? (similarities, contrasts, cause and effect) What meaning or truth does each connection point out?_____
_____
_____
_____
_____
_____

What is the BIG truth this passage is teaching? Write it in one sentence._____

_____

_____

_____

_____

_____

What is the main thing the Lord is saying to me through this chapter? (something to obey? A truth about Him I can rejoice in? A promise I can take for a situation I'm in?)_____

_____

_____

_____

_____

_____

_____

_____

Further insights:_____

_____

_____

_____

_____

_____

_____

Other related passages (Search for related texts by cross reference and concordance):_____

_____

_____

_____

_____

_____

_____

_____

What is Orthodox Christianity?

Jesus is God. His Word, the Bible is true. We do not have to soft-pedal the Lordship of Jesus Christ. He is to be obeyed. Period. Many Christians have different viewpoints on things such as baptism, worship music style, or what names they give to church leadership. There is however a core of beliefs that define "Orthodox Christianity." All that simply means is sticking to the Biblical viewpoints of the essentials of the faith. Here is a list of beliefs that Christians adhere to. Do not compromise on these truths.

1. There is only one God eternally existent in the triune Godhead: God the Father, God the Son, and God the Holy Spirit.

2. Jesus Christ is the only begotten Son of the Father, eternally co-existing with Him from and beyond eternity. He was conceived by the Holy Spirit, was born of the Virgin Mary, was crucified, died, was buried, and rose again on the third day. He ascended in bodily form into Heaven where He awaits us, is seated at the right hand of the Father and is interceding for us.

3. God created the world and all that is in it. He has ownership rights over all people because He created them.

4. All people have sinned and fall short of the glory of God. The wages of sin is death and eternity in hell.

5. Jesus Christ died on the cross as a substitute, receiving the punishment we deserve (propitiation). Forgiveness of sin (salvation), new life (redemption), and a right relationship with God (justification) are all available to people because of the cross. These gifts are received by faith in Jesus Christ.

6. The Holy Spirit sets us apart (sanctification) to be holy. He fills us and empowers us to live godly lives so we can take the Gospel to the ends of the earth.

7. There will be a resurrection of the dead and a Day of Judgment. All people will acknowledge that Jesus is Lord. Those who believe will experience eternal life with Jesus forever. Those who rejected Jesus will spend eternity in hell.

8. The Holy Bible is the only inspired and authoritative Word of God, without error and fully trustworthy, speaking to all of life: the church, the family, the government, economics, history, and relationships.

MEREDITH CURTIS

Powerline Productions

Being World Changers!

Raising World Changers!

Powerline Productions exists to serve you! We want you to grow in your relationship with Jesus, experience joy and success in your homeschooling journey, and fulfill the Great Commission with your family in your home, church, and community. We offer Homeschooling books, unit studies, classes, high school courses, ladies Bible studies, God's Girls Bible studies, Real Men discipleship manuals, and cookbooks just for you!

Our Websites

powerlineprod.com/
meredithcurtis.com/
joyfulandsuccessfulhomeschooling.com/
jshomeschooling.com/
finishwellcon.com/

E-books Available at powerlineprod.com/
payhip.com/powerlineproductions
currclick.com/browse/pub/247/Powerline-Productions

Print Books Available @ amazon.com/ **(look up Books by Title)**

Kindle Books Available @ amazon.com/ **(look up Books by Title)**

Contact Us: Laura@powerlinecc.com **&** Meredith@powerlinecc.com **&**
PastorMike@powerlinecc.com

Powerline Productions
251 Brightview Drive Lake Mary, FL 32746

Homeschooling High School to the Glory of God

If your homeschooling journey includes high school and you are looking classes or for some ideas on designing your own classes, then you are the person I am writing for. This series is for you and your family!

When my oldest daughter was 12, I began planning her high school curriculum. There were so many things on my heart for her to learn, books I wanted her to read, and dreams I had for her high school education. I designed her entire high school curriculum. This curriculum has been adapted for the rest of my children and Laura's children. We have worked hard to give our children the best classes possible.

My classes have been, are, and will be adapted to every child to fit their own needs and designed to take advantage of opportunities that arise, such as coop classes, vacations, and seminars. This series is simply my philosophy of educating my high school children at home, along with classes we have used in our family over the years. Hopefully, you will be inspired to create your own classes! Or, you can adapt my classes however you would like to! After all, you are the teacher!

My goal for high school is to provide a general education that can be a springboard to any and every possible career and education path that exists for my children. That is a HUGE goal, so I may not reach it, but if I aim for nothing I'll hit nothing, so I am aiming for something BIG! With that in mind, I try to cultivate and develop gifts, talents, and goals. I don't expect my teenager to know what he/she is going to want to do for the rest of his/her life, so I try to prepare for ALL possibilities.

Here is our family's *God's Girls 105: Homemaking* course. I hope you and your high school children will enjoy it as much as we have. May it be a blessing! Feel free to adapt this class any way you want to. After all, you are the teacher.

This is the just one of the classes in the Homeschooling to the Glory of God series. There are more classes and collections of classes available and coming soon.

Here is a list of individual classes that are available now!

- *New Testament Survey*
- *Old Testament Survey*
- *Worldview 101: Understand the Times*
- *Great Commission*
- *Web Design 101*
- *Economics, Personal Finances, & Business*
- *HIS Story of the 20th Century with High School Workbook*
- *Government: God's Blueprint/Man's Agenda*
- *British Literature & Writing*
- *American Literature & Research*
- *Who-Dun-It Murder Mystery*
- *Foundations of Western Literature*
- *Communication 101: Essays & Speeches*
- *Songwriting 101: Make a Joyful Noise*

- *Real Men 101: Godly Manhood*
- *Real Men 102: Freedom, Courtship, Marriage, and Family*
- *Real Men 103: Leadership Class*
- *Real Men 104: Pass the Torch*
- *God's Girls 101: Grow in Christ*
- *God's Girls 102: Virtuous Womanhood*
- *God's Girls 103: Courtship, Marriage, & The Christian Family*
- *God's Girls 104: Motherhood*
- *God's Girls 105: Homemaking*
- *God's Girls 106: Friendship, Hospitality, & Celebrations*
- *God's Girls 107: How to Homeschool*

Here is a list of current books in the series:

- *Unlocking the Mysteries of Credits, Classes, & Transcripts*
- *Teaching Literature in High School with Classes You Can Use*
- *Teaching Writing in High School with Classes You Can Use*

Here is a list of upcoming books in the series:

- *Teaching Bible in High School with Classes You Can Use*
- *Teaching Character & Life Skills in High School with Classes You Can Use*
- *Teaching History & Geography in High School with Classes You Can Use*
- *Teaching Government in High School with Classes You Can Use*
- *Teaching Math & Science in High School with Classes You Can Use*
- *Teaching Art, Music, & Drama in High School with Classes You Can Use*
- *Teaching Economics, Business & Personal Finances in High School with Classes You Can Use*
- *Teaching Physical Education & Health in High School with Classes You Can Use*
- *Teaching Homemaking in High School with Classes You Can Use*

Happy Homeschooling! And remember to Homeschool to the Glory of God!

Meredith Ludwig Curtis

God's Girls Bible Studies

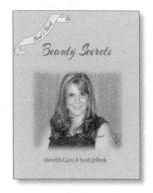   

God's Girls Classes

High School Classes

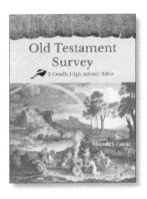

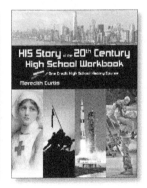

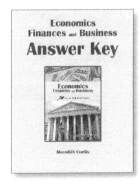

Maggie King Mysteries

  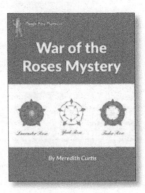 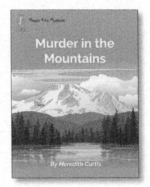

Ladies Bible Studies

  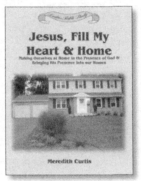 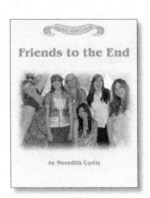

More Books from Powerline Production

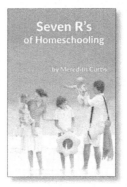

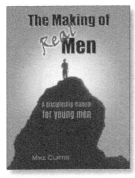

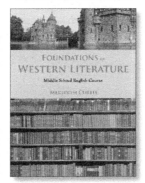

More Books from Powerline Production

 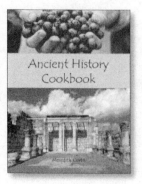  

 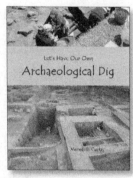  

   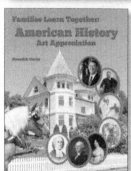

 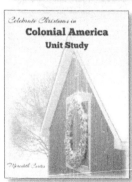 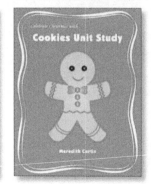 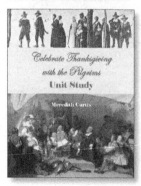

About the Author

 Meredith Curtis, a pastor's wife and homeschooling mom of five children, leads worship, mentors ladies, and, sometimes, even cooks dinner. Her passion is to equip people to love Jesus, raise godly children, and change the world around them with the power of the Gospel. "Lives are changed in the context of relationships," Meredith often says, as well as, "Be a world changer! Raise world changers!" She enjoys speaking to small and large groups.

All inquiries can be made to the author, Meredith Curtis, through email: Meredith@powerlinecc.com or contact her through her websites:
joyfulandsuccessfulhomeschooling.com/
meredithcurtis.com/
finishwellcon.com/
powerlineprod.com/

Meredith is the author of several books.
Joyful and Successful Homeschooling
Seven R's of Homeschooling
Quick & EZ Unit Study Fun
Unlocking the Mysteries of Homeschooling High School (with Laura Nolette)
Celebrate Thanksgiving
Teaching Writing in High School with Classes You Can Use
Teaching Literature in High School with Classes You Can Use
HIS Story of the 20th Century
HIS Story of the 20th Century for Little Folks

Meredith is the author of several cozy mysteries: The Maggie King Mysteries series.
Drug Dealers Deadly Disguise
Hurricanes Can Be Deadly
Legend of the Candy Cane Murder
Wash, Dry, Cut, & Die
War of the Roses Mystery
Murder in the Mountains

Meredith is the author of several Bible studies.
Lovely to Behold
A Wise Woman Builds
Jesus, Fill My Heart & Home
Welcome Inn: Practicing the Art of Hospitality in Jesus" Name
Friends to the End
God's Girls Beauty Secrets (with Sarah Jeffords)
God's Girls Friends to the End (with Katie-Beth Nolette & Sarah Jeffords)

God's Girls Talk about Boys, Dating, Courtship, & Marriage

Meredith is the author of several unit studies, timelines, and cookbooks.
Celebrate Christmas in Colonial America
Celebrate Christmas with Cookies
Travel to London
Celebrate Thanksgiving with the Pilgrims
American History Cookbook
Ancient History Cookbook
20ᵗʰ Century Cookbook (with Laura Nolette)
20ᵗʰ Century Timeline (with Laura Nolette)
American History Timeline (with Laura Nolette)
Ancient History Timeline (with Laura Nolette)
Let's Have Our Own Medieval Banquet (with Laura Nolette)
Let's Have Our Archaeological Dig
Let's Have Our Own Olympic Games

Meredith is the author of several high school classes.
American Literature and Research
British Literature and Writing
Who Dun It: Murder Mystery Literature & Writing
Communication 101: Essays and Speeches
Foundations of Western Literature
Economics, Finances, and Business
Government: God's Blueprint/Man's Agenda
HIS Story of the 20ᵗʰ Century with HIS Story of the 20ᵗʰ Century High School Workbook
Worldview 101: Understand the Times
New Testament Survey
Old Testament Survey
Great Commission
Career Choices and The College Decision
Real Men 101: Godly Manhood
Real Men 102: Freedom, Courtship, Marriage, and Family
Real Men 103: Leadership
Real Men 104: Pass the Torch
God's Girls 101: Grow in Christ
God's Girls 102: Virtuous Womanhood
God's Girls 103: Courtship, Marriage, and the Christian Family
God's Girls 104: Motherhood
God's Girls 105: Homemaking
God's Girls 106: Friendship, Hospitality, and Celebrations
God's Girls 107: How to Homeschool

And more…

Made in the USA
Monee, IL
08 August 2021

75196376R00201